John Richardson Illingworth

**University and cathedral sermons**

John Richardson Illingworth

**University and cathedral sermons**

ISBN/EAN: 9783744745444

Printed in Europe, USA, Canada, Australia, Japan

Cover: Foto ©Lupo / pixelio.de

More available books at **www.hansebooks.com**

# UNIVERSITY

AND

# CATHEDRAL SERMONS

BY

J. R. ILLINGWORTH, M.A.

AUTHOR OF 'SERMONS PREACHED IN A COLLEGE CHAPEL'

London
MACMILLAN AND CO
AND NEW YORK
1893

# CONTENTS

|  |  | PAGE |
|---|---|---|
| I. | Conduct and Creed | 1 |
| II. | The Son the Way to the Father | 21 |
| III. | (The) Service of the Heart | 39 |
| IV. | (The) Service of the Mind | 57 |
| V. | (The) Service of the Soul | 72 |
| VI. | God's Love the Cause of Ours | 87 |
| VII. | Innocence | 99 |
| VIII. | Vocation | 120 |
| IX. | (The) Captivity of Thought | 144 |
| X. | Prayer | 164 |
| XI. | (The) Incarnation of the Word | 181 |
| XII. | The Risen Life | 208 |

Of the following sermons, Nos. I. II. VII. VIII. IX. were preached before the University of Oxford; No. XI. before the University of Cambridge; Nos. III. IV. V. VI. XII. in St. Paul's Cathedral; and No. X. in Westminster Abbey.

# I

## CONDUCT AND CREED

"Be ye therefore perfect, even as your Father which is in heaven is perfect."—ST. MATT. v. 48.

AMONG the many "old orders" which are nowadays thought to be "giving place to new," not the least important is that "old order" which for centuries has identified the highest morality with the following of the faith of Christ. Religion and morality, we are told by our primitive historians, were independent in their origins and in the earlier stages of their development, and though in the dark ages popular morality could only be aroused by religious motives and enforced by religious sanctions, the alliance, we are assured, was after all but an unholy one; and the time is coming, as for enlightened minds it has already come, when conduct is to reassert its freedom from religious interference, and its native superiority to religious hope or fear. And in this, as in all other ages of intellectual transition, men are liable to renounce their belief in the old order prematurely, before they have attained a confident conviction of the new. In the practical affairs of life we are awake to the danger of such a proceeding: a mountaineer does not leave his handhold till his foothold is secure; a man of business does not retire till he has provided for his future; an unjust steward is wise enough to falsify his accounts before his dismissal. But in the far deeper regions of the political, the moral, the spiritual life, all this is too often reversed, and men let go with a strange improvidence their hold upon convictions which, however inadequate, have been powerfully real in the past, only to clutch at empty nothingness and die shattered in the abyss.

The question therefore of the relation between Christianity and moral conduct is for all who profess and call themselves, in any sense of the word, Christians, far more fundamental, and at the present moment far more vitally important, than any of the minor anxieties which now exercise the religious world. Men only forget that this is so because they are at present in possession of a body of moral rules and principles which have come to be regarded as axiomatic, and for daily purposes practically complete. But this body of morality is an inheritance from the Christian past, and the spiritual momentum of the Christian past is upon it. If we look beyond it to the ethical questions which are still unsolved, or in process of solution—for example, those which concern the laws of marriage, the moral responsibility of nations in their collective capacity, the equity of capital and labour, the limit of the rights of conscience, the moral character of intellectual assent, the degree of human authority over the animal creation—we see at once that the first principles upon which these questions are being discussed are often strangely at variance with those upon which the body of our morality has been established, and capable, if granted, of acting retrospectively and disintegrating the very moral axioms of the past. In view therefore of this chaos, and of the havoc which its contemplation is now working in countless individual souls, we must not forget that Christianity has a moral system of its own, which claims to have the same relation to what may be called "Natural Ethics" that Revelation has to Natural Religion or "Natural Theology," and that

> We needs must love the highest when we see it.

The fact that, in the earlier ages of human evolution, religion and morality were often entirely apart, and that their primitive severance has left its traces upon Hebrew as on other history, is no way inconsistent with the Christian belief that, in and by the Incarnation, they were once and for all time united, and a new species thereby developed in the spiritual world.

> All tended to mankind,
> And, man produced, all has its end thus far:
> But in completed man begins anew
> A tendency to God. Prognostics told

> Man's near approach ; so in man's self arise
> August anticipations, symbols, types
> Of a dim splendour ever on before
> In that eternal circle life pursues.

And our wider modern views of history do, therefore, but lay increasing emphasis upon the old speculation of the Franciscan theologians, who regarded the Incarnation as being, independently of its other aspects, the predestined, and therefore natural consummation, of our race; the birth of "a new creature" by the one act, as we might now phrase it, of creative evolution, which has been done before the eyes of men. Throughout pre-Christian civilisation the philosophic few either ignored religion, or deigned to dally with it doubtfully, and failed, therefore, to carry their high morality home to the hearts of men ; while the masses strove to shelter their laxity of conduct under the shadow of some more or less immoral superstition : and the essential novelty of Christianity, when viewed from the side of human history, was its presentation of a new life, in which creed and conduct were intimately, indissolubly, necessarily one. The Sermon on the Mount is often regarded as merely a code of morality which may be isolated with advantage from the metaphysics of the Christian creed. But if we regard the Sermon on the Mount as merely a moral code, we are at once struck by its intense, its impracticable idealism.

"Blessed are the poor in spirit," "If thy right eye offend thee, pluck it out," "Resist not evil," "Give to him that asketh of thee," "Love your enemies," "Take no thought for the morrow," "Judge not," "Be ye perfect"—these and the like commandments, however much they may have been anticipated in India, or practised by Essene recluses, or thought out independently by Stoics here and there, are in too defiant contradiction of the apparent laws of social progress ever to have commanded the assent of the most practical portion of our race, except in the conscious assurance of a super-human law under the human paradox, a divine power under the human will. And it is to this assurance that the whole of the Sermon on the Mount appeals. "Let your light shine before men . . . that they may glorify your Father," " Love your enemies . . . that ye may be the children of your Father," " Pray to thy Father which seeth in secret," " Take no thought for your life . . . for your heavenly Father knoweth that ye have need," " When ye pray, say Our Father," " Be ye perfect, even as your Father." The existence of a Divine Father, and our capacity for communion with Him, is the necessary postulate and presupposition of the Sermon on the Mount. And this fact at once characterises the Christian system as one of "absolute morality." " Be ye perfect, even as your Father is perfect." It puts before us an absolutely perfect Being as the ultimate standard for our conduct, condemning us by that very fact to be, " when we have done all, unprofitable servants," but consecrating all our ideal aspirations, by assuring us that they are not the mere mental fringes of our experience as it fades into unknown space, but justifiable appropriations by anticipation of a reality now outside us, but in time destined to be ours. " Brethren, now are we the sons of God, and it doth not yet appear what we shall be; but we know that when He shall appear we shall be like Him, for we shall see Him as He is."

But a speculative knowledge of the absolute is, we know, impossible to us, for "No man hath seen God at any time." What is possible is an inductive knowledge through experience, and it is to such knowledge that we are pointed in the Sermon on the Mount. "Consider the lilies of the field, how they grow; they toil not, neither do they spin;" "Wherefore, if God so clothe the grass of the field, shall He not much more clothe you?" "He maketh His sun to rise on the evil and on the good, and sendeth rain on the just and on the unjust;" "Be ye therefore perfect, even as your Father which is in heaven is perfect;" "If ye, being evil, know how to give good gifts unto your children, how much more shall your Father which is in heaven give good things to them that ask Him;"—it is to the laws of nature and of human character that we are here referred for our knowledge of God; and no scientific distinction can be drawn between these two sources of information. The superficial plausibility of the criticism which accepts the notions of God which are derived from the laws of nature, as being scientific, and rejects those which are derived from the laws of human character, as being anthropomorphic, is solely due to the interfering presence of sin in the latter case—"Ye being evil." But the presence of sin does not vitiate, it only obscures the evidence; and when once in human history there had appeared a character in which could be found no fault, it became thenceforward and for ever strictly scientific to derive notions of God from that human personality, which is the highest object within present experience; and to conclude that our Father which is in heaven, however much in the language of the day He may transcend personality, must yet at least be as much as personal, and therefore be more adequately represented in the mind of Christ than in the laws which govern the inanimate creation—as man is above the sunrise, and the fowls of the air, and the lilies of the field.

"No man hath seen God at any time . . . the only begotten Son He hath declared Him." "Philip saith unto Him, Lord, show us the Father. . . . Jesus saith unto him, Have I been so long time with you, and yet hast thou not known Me, Philip? He that hath seen Me, hath seen the Father." "No man cometh unto the Father but by Me."

Christianity therefore not only provides us with an absolute *end* for conduct, which, as being real, makes our moral ideals speculatively justifiable—but it provides us with an adequate knowledge of that end in the teaching and character and life and death of Jesus Christ—that is, with a *standard* for conduct, which, as having been realised in human history, makes our moral ideals practically possible. If the Sermon on the Mount had been and remained a code of ethics, written upon tables of stone, it might have been liable to the charges of inadequacy and of exaggeration which have been so often brought against it. But it is part of a whole, and needs the interpretation of its Author's life to be taken with it—πατρὸς δεῖται βοηθοῦ. Its Author lived it to the bitter end — loving, resisting not evil, exceeding the righteousness of the Scribes and Pharisees, taking no thought for the morrow, judging no man; and, accepting the logical conclusion of His own intense moral idealism, scorn, solitude, the cross. No; in the face of the life of Jesus Christ it is wilful perversity to call the Sermon on the Mount exaggerated. In the face of the fruits of His death it is impossible to call it inadequate; or to deny that the gradual amelioration of our servile, our domestic, our social, our political, our intellectual, our moral life was all contained by implication in the precept "Be ye perfect," and has been wrought out under the influence of the Christian faith in obedience to the Christian sanction.

For beside its *end* and its *standard*, Christianity has a *sanction* of its own :—" That ye may be the children of your Father," "And your Father which seeth in secret shall reward you openly." We have outgrown the form of religious utilitarianism which attempted to enforce morality by an acute sense of benefits to come ; but we have not yet outlived the discredit into which that system dragged the religious sanction, and which gave rise to the popular modern fallacy that ethics and religion are best apart.

But for the Christian this separation is impossible. Of course there may be many subordinate sanctions, political, physical, or other, obliging us to this or that particular action or forbearance ; precisely as there may be minor maxims, under the general precept of perfection. But all these derive their authority from, and in case of conflict must be corrected by, the ultimate Christian sanction ; union, communion, fellowship, with the Father through the Son—an eternally present relationship, into which temporal distinctions do not enter. " He that hath the Son hath life, and he that hath not the Son hath not life."

It is legitimate, and in some cases necessary, to wake an unenlightened imagination by presenting this sanction under the forms of space and time, and appealing to the present and future consequences of moral evil, in order to force its intrinsic malignity into clearer relief; but in doing so we must remember that the consequences do not constitute but only exhibit the true nature of the evil, which consists essentially in our present separation from the source of life—"He that hath not the Son hath not life." And here extra-Christian criticism meets us with the objection, why appeal, in so vitally practical a matter, to a sanction which is mystical and, if not unreal, at least beyond the reach of experimental verification? We answer, because that sanction has been verified in history as the only adequate *motive* of the hearts and wills of men. Aristotle knew well the limitations of natural ethics when he prefaced his great treatise with the mournful admission, that it was useless for the young in years or in character—useless for all upon whom the hope of the future rested— useless to stem the lawless passions which were already hurrying Greece to that last chapter of its history which was written by St. Paul. Jesus Christ was not less experienced in human character when He said, "Suffer little children to come unto Me, for of such is the kingdom of heaven," secure in the power of His love to give the victory throughout the ages to the childlike spirit that alone can out of weakness be made strong. Ethics are nothing if not practical; and all the ethical systems of antiquity failed simply and solely for lack of a motive force. They did what they could, the philosophers, the law, and the prophets. They were necessary stages in the evolution of morality, at sundry times and in divers manners, till in the fulness of time Christ came, not to destroy, but to fulfil. Thenceforward religion and morality became, as we have seen, identified, in the belief that the ultimate end of conduct is union with the Father through the Son, and therefore necessitates the co-operation of His Spirit from above. That is, the third essential of the Christian system of ethics is the belief in a Spirit permanently present in the world, convincing it of sin, of righteousness, of judgment; interpreting the example, and continuing the work of the Incarnation in the individual and in the race.

"I have yet many things to say unto you, but ye cannot bear them now. Howbeit when He, the Spirit of truth, is come, He will guide you into all truth: . . . for He shall receive of mine, and shall show it unto you." And this doctrine of the Spirit is the Christian answer to the vexed question of the nature and origin of the moral faculty. We are familiar with the many efforts that have been made to defend the absolute character of morality, in face of the experimental philosophy, by postulating, under one name or other, an unique moral faculty; and of the plausible attempts of modern science to analyse that faculty into elements which are not moral. But to the Christian moralist the question is unessential; for he rests not on our power to apprehend the absolute, but on the power of the absolute to comprehend us. "The wind bloweth where it listeth, and thou hearest the sound thereof, but canst not tell whence it cometh, and whither it goeth: so is every one that is born of the Spirit." And though such spiritual influence is beyond speculative explanation, it is as open to inductive verification as any other of the ultimate laws of science, which are only known by their effects. Look at the fruit of the Spirit—love, joy, peace, longsuffering, gentleness, goodness, faith, meekness, temperance—as it has been shown through eighteen centuries in the lives of individual Christians, and through their lives in the customs and laws and institutions of society; modifying and moulding them, by gradual development, into closer harmony with the law of love which is "the mind of Christ"; and remember that men cannot gather grapes of thorns or figs of thistles.

Christianity therefore confronts the modern world with the claim to possess an ethical system, which gathered up into itself and fulfilled all that was true in bygone philosopher or prophet, which has led us on to the moral level upon which now we stand; and which is capable of infinite development in time to come; till the law of love is at length realised, and we all attain to "the measure of the stature of the fulness of Christ." But this claim rests entirely upon the strength of the combination between the Christian conduct and the Christian creed. That combination made possible what without it had been found impossible; and we have yet to learn that any modern extra-Christian system can succeed, where Moses and the prophets, where Plato and Aristotle failed. Of course in the lapse of ages much that is non-essential has slowly grown incorporate both in conduct and in creed. The moral law of love must of necessity embody itself in subordinate moral maxims, to meet new cases as they arise; and the faith of Christ must of necessity clothe itself in formulæ borrowed from and limited by the language of their age. And every generation of men, in its weary yearning after rest, strives to invest its own maxims and formulæ with an impossible finality, and to see in all that would surpass them, not fulfilment but destruction. Now as ever, therefore, there is work for Christian philosopher and prophet to follow the example of the Sermon on the Mount in distinguishing between letter and spirit, accident and essence—

> Faith in the thing, grown faith in the report,
> Whence need to bravely disbelieve report—
> Through increased faith in thing reports belie?
>
> .   .   .   .   .
>
> Correct the portrait by the living face,
> Man's God, by God's God in the mind of man.

This is a work of increasing delicacy and difficulty in a complex age like ours, when both in opinion and practice good and evil are often inextricably, indistinguishably interwoven; and a work not less certain now than of old to reward its workers with the benediction of being persecuted falsely. But it is a necessary work, if the dependence of morality upon Christianity is to be maintained. For "development" is the phrase of the day, and we measure the vitality of an organisation by its power of adapting itself to new conditions, expanding in new atmospheres, appropriating, assimilating, utilising new customs and ideas, evoking new capacities from within to answer each new call upon it from without. The moral system of Christianity has possessed this power in the past, and claims to possess it for the future, in a far more adequate degree than any of the secular systems which have grown up and flourished in the shadow of it, and embodied in their various watchwords of liberty, or utility, or happiness, or sacrifice, or self-development, partial and imperfect expressions of the perfect law of Love. But this morality, as we have seen, is what it is, simply and solely in virtue of its union with a faith which has also proved its own vitality, by permanent persistence, under varying and opposite conditions of persecution and of patronage, of ignorant and enlightened ages, of antagonistic forms of government and forms of society and forms of thought, and is no less capable now than ever of bringing forth things new and old, and becoming all things to all men.

The distinction, therefore, of spirit from letter, both in morality and creed, necessary as it is at all times, is, if possible, more necessary now; for it justifies, in the region of theory, the claim of Christianity to an eternal interest and influence in the evolution of our race; and by clearing its central verities from the battle-cloud of ages, it strengthens the force of our insistance upon the practical necessity of refusing to separate morality, not only in the pulpit, but whensoever and wheresoever and under what name soever it is taught at all, from the faith which has alone been able to give it might and meaning in the past.

The increasing pressure of the struggle for material existence, in which the masses of men are now engaged, threatens in the future to make pause for independent thought more and more impossible. Yet none the less the eternal issues of spiritual life and death are being invisibly fought out behind the chaos of the earthly conflict. There is need, therefore, now if ever, to point men to the Sermon on the Mount, with all its infinite unworldliness of precept and of promise, and to ask them, as they hurry by us in their struggle for success, "Who is he that overcometh the world, but he that believeth that Jesus is the Son of God?"

## II

## THE SON THE WAY TO THE FATHER

"Jesus saith unto him, I am the way, the truth, and the life: no man cometh unto the Father, but by me."—ST. JOHN xiv. 6.

THE belief in a Divine Father, to whom our conduct has relation, differentiates at once and for ever religious from secular morality. A morality built upon the experience of what is best in human character, and bent on eliciting from that experience the utmost attainable perfection, may astonish us by the nobility, the purity, the beauty of its results. But it revolves round a wholly different centre from, and in a far less ample circuit than, that of the man who looks beyond himself to a power more than human, which alone understands his unfelt capacities, his real surroundings, his unknown destiny, and can alone, therefore, be entrusted with the intimate conduct of his life. It is the difference between the Ptolemaic and the Copernican astronomy.

But the Christian looks further again beyond this, the common horizon of all religions, to a Father, who is not only intelligent, powerful, pitiful, but of whose character, so far as it can be apprehended by the human intellect, he has an adequate knowledge through the revelation of His Son; and to whom he believes himself to be vitally, organically bound, by the indwelling of a Divine Spirit that can alone enable his human weakness to breathe the air of heaven. And it is this closeness of relation to a God, who is thus both an object of knowledge to our intellect and a subject of experience to our heart, that gives its peculiar difference, not only to the Christian character regarded as a whole, but also to each one of its component virtues in detail. The isolated precepts of the Sermon on the Mount are peculiar to no one religion. It is in the faith upon which they are founded, and the confidence that such faith alone can give, that their Christian character and their practicability alike consist. In other words, the moral life of the Christian is as inseparable from the spiritual as are the chemical changes in a plant or animal from the vital forces which control them. If we attempt to treat it independently, it will dwindle into a mere abstraction. The famous picture of the dignified man who is greatly worthy, and at the same time greatly conscious of his worth, was a noble one, and fruitful of many a high Stoic life and death of calm resolve. But it was wholly different in kind from the spirit that enabled St. Paul to say, "I live, yet not I, Christ liveth in me." "Not that we are sufficient of ourselves to think anything as of ourselves, but our sufficiency is of God." "I can do all things through Christ which strengtheneth me." The moral philosophy of Greece and Rome was, as we know, their whole religion; and yet it made few great lives possible, and passed away with the stately sadness of a dying aristocrat of the old régime, retiring in pathetic impotence from the vulgar contact of the religion that was destined to "make all things new." We may imitate its example to-day, but it will only be to share its fate.

The thought, therefore, of a present God, one who knows us, loves us, desires us, co-operates with our efforts, is essential to our practice of the Christian virtues. But we are living at the present time in an intellectual atmosphere from which that thought has been, to a large extent, eliminated. The consequence is that a large number, if not a majority, of professing Christians have adopted a morality which is no longer distinctively Christian. Their speculative belief, it is true, may have remained unchanged, but the disintegrating influence of this subtle, impalpable, pervasive, corrosive, atmosphere has loosened, without their knowledge, the bond of their conduct to their creed; and they live, and move, and act, in practical affairs without feeling from day to day the need of the Divine co-operation, the force of the Divine attraction, the constraint of the Divine love. But dangers which elude us by their subtlety do not cease to be dangerous. If what is called Agnosticism were the exclusive characteristic of obvious antagonists in well-defined array, it would be no very new enemy to the Church of Christ. But modern Agnosticism is nothing of this kind; it is a shifting, shapeless mist that now covers our enemies, and now our friends, and now hides the true nature of the battle-ground between us. It means a hundred things in the mouths of a hundred different men. It is now a synonym for Atheism, and now the chosen weapon of the Christian apologist, and we must therefore, if we would clear our conduct from the spell of this miasmic influence, force the word to give an account of itself, and tell us what it means.

Strictly interpreted, the word Agnosticism should be confined to the position of those who maintain that there is no evidence in the empirical and experimental sciences, when taken by themselves, to prove or to disprove the existence of a God. But such a doctrine, to say the least of it, is in no way incompatible with the Christian belief in a God whom no man hath seen at any time; who is not in the fire, or the whirlwind, or the earthquake; whose ways are not as our ways; and who cannot be found out by searching among the things of the natural world. The natural world has always been patient of two interpretations, and cannot at its utmost do more than witness to the workings of a God the conviction of whose existence is derived from other sources. And the imagination which is exclusively exercised upon physical phenomena, must as inevitably, now as of old, draw the conclusions of Lucretius, precisely as in morals the mind that is absorbed by earthly images cannot escape the consequent sensuality of life. It is from the evidence of conscience, and from the evidence of consciousness, that men have in all ages drawn their belief in God; and consciousness and conscience, despite all question-begging efforts to unravel them, are the same to-day that they once were for Aristotle and for Plato, for David and Isaiah, and for Felix when he trembled. If, therefore, Agnosticism were confined to the opinion that physical science in the abstract can have no theological bearings, it would be as true as a similar statement in respect of his own department when made by a political economist or pure mathematician. But in actual fact it means more than this; it is the courteous disclaimer of a practised controversialist, who, while he declines the attempt to prove a negative, insinuates his conviction that, after all, with sufficient diligence a negative might be proved. And this illegitimate extension of Agnostic doctrine slowly overcasts the moral and religious life with an almost imperceptible cloud of insecurity, till men find, when duty calls them, or temptation presses hard, that without any conscious change of attitude, they have lost their old reliance upon God. For, say what men will, probability is not the guide of the religious life. "I know in whom I have believed" has been the motto of the Christian heroes; they could not have achieved their conquests in the faith of a "great perhaps." If, therefore, we would live the Christian life, in the power of the Christian faith by which alone it can be lived, we must be awake and aware of the insidious danger of our daily contact with Agnostic opinion. Agnostic opinion, if it is not to be a euphemism for a less popular word, is only legitimate if anywhere in the region of physical science; though even beyond the dim border-land of our present physical science, we are beginning to catch a glimpse of strange forces and potencies and modes of being which suggest that we are still " moving about in worlds not realised," and that possibilities of knowledge await us which are practically infinite ; and few sane men would nowadays venture to maintain that there is not room in that unknown region for the whole compass of the Christian creed. So much may fairly be maintained in argument with those who do not share in our belief. But as Christians, for our own assurance, we can go further still, for we, too, possess an experimental science, fruitful as any other, in positive results. It is the science of the spiritual life. The great mysteries of life and death, and sin, and sorrow, and temptation have been breaking hearts and wrecking minds from the dawn of human history. And one body of men, and one only, have met, and faced, and overcome them, the body of believers in the revelation of the Son of God. Statesmen and slaves, kings and philosophers, women and children, old and young, have shown themselves in every age, by lives of sanctity and deaths of martyrdom, possessors of the secret of spiritual success; and by every law of evidence we are bound to give them credit, when they tell us with one accord, amid every difference of rank and age, "this is the victory which overcometh the world, even our faith." We must not be deluded into thinking that the world's belief in the revelation of the God of love rests, or has ever rested, on the hallucinations of a few enthusiasts. It rests upon the evidence of countless witnesses in countless ages, witnesses of unquestioned sanity, witnesses of transparent probity, and who have not shrunk from supplementing, in modern phrase, their observation by experiment, that is, from trusting their whole lives to the Divine influence which they have felt within them: with the result of acquiring an insight, a power, and a peace which have never been attained by other means or other men. These have been the true professors of spiritual science, and the field of their experience has been as open for two thousand years as it is to-day. For that field is the soul of man, seen in the sunlight fire of the Cross of Christ. To say that such knowledge is mystical is only true in the sense that it cannot be reached or tested by the methods of any other science. It is not mystical in the sense of being incommunicable, for it can be communicated to each and all who will follow its invitation to come and see. We know the difference between the sciolist who plays with thoughts that are not his own, and the man who has lavished upon his science the love and labour of a lifetime; and it is reasonable that there should be the same distinction between the external critic of a religious doctrine, and the man who has had the courage to forego all things for its sake—

The vulgar saw thy tower, thou saw'st the sun.

A scientific expert justly resents lay interference with his methods of inquiry or the value of his results. A Christian may not less justly claim that the truths which he holds for certain, and the methods of their acquisition should alike be judged of from within, especially when he remembers that, apart from intellectual opposition, the imperious nature of the control which his religion claims to exercise over the personal life of man must inevitably enlist against it the whole weight of the moral bias of its own half-hearted adherents.

But beyond the scientific Agnosticism, which may be granted in its own sphere to be legitimate, we live among forms of what may be called religious Agnosticism; that is, forms of thought which, while retaining a minimum of what is supposed to be requisite to constitute a religion, surrender, in false deference to the spirit of the age, as large a portion as they think possible of the metaphysics of their creed, —in unconsciousness that by so doing they empty it of moral significance as well. These attempts are retrogressive; counter to the spirit of development; and a Christian may reasonably maintain that such systems are self-condemned by their mutual exclusiveness; while Christianity includes them, as a late complex result of evolution includes the succession of simpler elements which it has incorporated in itself.

Three such mutilations of religion are popular in the educated opinion of the present day. Two of them, Theism and Pantheism, profess equally with Christianity to hold, at least, speculative opinions upon that which transcends experience, and do not therefore in reality gain any advantage over Christianity by their partial surrender of the metaphysical supports which must be abandoned wholly or not at all.

Theism, or Monotheism, as it is sometimes miscalled, clings solely to the thought that we have a Father who is in heaven, whom in our misery and helplessness we can trust implicitly to comfort and sustain us, by the very fact that He sitteth above the water-floods of all our chance and change, and never sleepeth or needs to be awakened.

"Thou, Lord, in the beginning hast laid the foundation of the earth, and the heavens are the work of Thy hands. They shall perish, but Thou shalt endure; they all shall wax old as doth a garment; and as a vesture shalt Thou change them, and they shall be changed. But Thou art the same, Thy years shall not fail." That is the truth of Theism.

But it is not the whole truth. However favourably such a creed may contrast in India with less pure faiths, it cannot claim with justice to be the vanguard of religious advance in Europe, and should more fairly be known by its older and negative name of Deism—for it involves the negation of one-half of the religious consciousness, and it is to that no less important instinct that Pantheism clings. For Pantheism does cling to no less important an instinct of our race, to

> A sense sublime
> Of something far more deeply interfused,
> Whose dwelling is the light of setting suns,
> And the round ocean and the living air,
> And the blue sky, and in the mind of man,
> A motion and a spirit that impels
> All thinking things, all objects of all thought
> And rolls through all things,

the conviction that there is a Presence in the groaning and travailing creation; strangely akin to that Spirit which we feel striving with our spirit and convincing us of sin, "I am a worm and no man," because He convinces us of righteousness. "I have said, Ye are gods; and ye are all the children of the most High;" "your bodies are the temples of the Holy Ghost."

Yet true as are the positive assertions of Theism and of Pantheism, they mutually exclude each other, and by so doing violate the completeness of the religious instinct; while the Christian position includes all that is positive in either, and therefore stands the test of probability, as being the more comprehensive of the three.

But there is another religious system which claims to lay all metaphysics aside, and to be the legitimate and final outcome of the religious consciousness of an Agnostic age. Fixing its thoughts solely on the brotherhood of man, it calls upon us, in the name of the religion of humanity, to leave all thought of the before and after, and whether there be a God or no, and confine ourselves to the service of our fellow-men. True religion, they would say, in borrowed language, is to bear one another's burdens, and to go about doing good; to visit the fatherless and widow in their afflictions, to rejoice with them that do rejoice, and weep with them that weep. It is a noble creed, and has attracted countless noble souls, long before a modern form of it was called by the name of Positivism; and a creed which might seem at first sight to have no relation to the Christian doctrine in virtue of its rejection of all metaphysic. Yet, strange to say, it is in truth more intimately connected with that doctrine than either of the systems we have previously reviewed. Theism and Pantheism are as old as recorded history; but the religion of humanity was the invention of Jesus Christ, and would never have survived the storms of the early ages to blossom in the modern world, except under the protecting shelter of the belief that Jesus Christ was God. Plato and Aristotle would have nothing to say to the religion of humanity. Hebrew exclusiveness and Roman pride could not together have created it. It was created by the Christian religion and sustained by the Christian love. And however true it may be that isolated men have, from time to time thereafter, exhibited its power, while denying the source from which it was unconsciously derived, the fact remains that it has never been a social force, except under the protection of the Christian creed. We have spoken of the Christian creed as containing and combining all that was true and real in Theism and in Pantheism. But, in the case of the religion of humanity, we may go further than this and say, that without belief in that doctrine it would never have existed, and without belief in that doctrine it will not continue to exist.

When, therefore, such currents of negative opinion, whether from the scientific or the religious side, threaten the confidence of our spiritual, and therefore of our moral life, we must distinguish between what it is to be the victims of intellectual refutation and a moral indolence that will not suffer us to realise our privileges and responsibilities, and which we are bound therefore to combat as we would any other temptation. Generations, like individuals, have each their besetting temptation, and ours is to think from the high level of our average morality, that we can live in less close and conscious dependence upon the Divine assistance than the men of old, who through that assistance raised our morality to what it is. We have special need, therefore, in the present day to remind ourselves from time to time that the specifically Christian virtues owe their essential character, their τί ἦν εἶναι, to our consciousness of the love of " our Father which is in heaven," of the revelation of that love on Calvary, and of our capacity for living in the power of it, in virtue of its own free self-communication to our souls; and that even the natural virtues, which we share with other systems, must be possessed by us in Aristotelian phrase κατ' ἄλλον τρόπον, not only as results of reasoning, but also as gifts of grace.

The days of penitence and humiliation are

now close upon us, and in their presence it is no spirit of intellectual trifling that seeks to enforce the moral importance of keeping our theology intact. It is by the death-bed, and in the despair of the fainting, failing, sin-scourged soul, that the Christian learns to value the metaphysics of his creed: when he feels that, however far they lie beyond the range of scientific experience, or the speculative simplicity of more elementary religions, they have been the means of the safe transmission of the knowledge of that love that along the ages has alone enabled the reconciled sinner to depart from earth in peace. And by all that that love has yet done, or shall ever do for us, we must remember that we are bound to hand on the knowledge of it as we have received it; the knowledge of the truth as it is in Jesus, without whom no man cometh to the Father.

## III

# THE SERVICE OF THE HEART

"Thou shalt love the Lord thy God with all thy heart."
ST. MATT. xxii. 37.

ALL men know, or think they know, what love is. The poets have sung its praises, and the philosophers have analysed it, and the moralists have assigned it a niche, under one name or other, among their virtues; but all have alike regarded it as too irrational, too capricious, too transitory a thing to be an adequate foundation for morality. Christianity alone has made love at once the guide and goal of life, the condition of perfection, the fulfilling of the law.

Now for the mass of men, who have neither time nor capacity to theorise, and yet who none the less desire to lead the higher life, the principle of love has an advantage over all the formulæ of the secular moralists, in being so *universal* that no heart is exempt from its sway; so indisputably *real* that no man can deny its influence; so quick with vital *energy* that, wherever it exists, it must issue in some form of action.

School after school of moralists, in their efforts to reach an universal formula for conduct, have landed themselves among phrases, which, to the average mind, were abstract and unreal, and needed elaborate justification at the bar of popular opinion before they could be brought into contact with the affairs of daily life; while even then there remained a gulf, which was helplessly, hopelessly impassable, between the moral rule and the moral force which was to put the rule in action. But the principle of love is universal, without being abstract, it is a fact, a plain, obvious, palpable reality, which all men agree to recognise, and to recognise as ultimate and fundamental. Its analogues are broadcast throughout the universe, from the laws of gravitation upwards. It is universal, it is real, and further, it is vital. It is its own dynamic. It lives and grows and expands and fructifies, and sows its fiery contagion broadcast with an importunate, an imperious necessity of its own inner nature, which admits of neither help nor hindrance from without. The command, therefore, to love appeals to an instinct which is co-extensive with humanity, which is real beyond touch of controversy, and endowed with a vital force that is exclusively its own. "Many waters cannot quench love, neither can the floods drown it."

But the very instinctive nature of love often misleads men into thinking that it is not a fit subject for command. Other things they say may be done or forborn in obedience to command, but love is as capricious and as free as air. This is a fallacy, which, like many other fallacies, owes its plausibility to its containing half a truth. Love is indeed irresistible; many waters cannot quench it. But like other irresistible forces—the lapse of a river, the electric energy, the current of a flame—it can be guided, and by guidance be controlled. "Learning to love" is too deep-set a phrase in our language ever to have arisen, if the act which it describes were after all impossible. St. John and St. Paul knew human nature, what it could do and what it could not do, when they said "Love not the world," and "Set your affections on things on high." And love, like the other instincts in a being that is rational, not only can be, but must be, directed by the will, as the sole condition of attaining its true end.

To assist us to that end let us look at love as we find it among men. In the first place, love is a relation existing between persons. The will need not have for its field of exercise more than a law, nor the mind more than an abstract object; but it is only in a derived and secondary sense that we can speak of loving anything other than a person. We may love him for the possession of this or that attribute of loveliness; but it is the self behind the attributes—the person—that we love. And then, though we cannot analyse this mysterious element of our being, we may see one thing about it clearly, that it moves between two poles—desire and sacrifice. The family, the earliest home of love, shows both these elements in their simplest form. The love of the child for the parent is one of simple, unreflective, self-referent desire; that of the parent for the child one of increasingly unselfish sacrifice. Both factors, of course, coexist, but in each case one predominates, and gives character and colour to the whole. And between these polar opposites all true love lives and moves—from the infant craving to make all objects of affection our own, to the love, than which no man hath greater, that a man lay down his life for his friends. The higher literature of the emotions is full of pictures of such love, but they do but reflect the experience of every human heart. We know, if we have ever loved at all, the intimate blending of these two elements, and how much depends, when they are in discord, upon the choice between them that is made. For there is a false love as well as a true; the love that travels backward from sacrifice to selfishness, and ends, if carried out consistently, in the hatred of its former objects, that is, in its own destruction, for hatred is the death of love. Remember the familiar history of Faust; the philosopher turning back in his old age from science to the sensual appetite he miscalls love; the downward course, the growing heartlessness, the ruin of the village maiden; and then, for this is only the first episode in such careers, follow him on to where the poet paints him with still profounder insight, calling to his arms the phantom Helen, the unreal image of sensual beauty, dead and buried long ago, in the vain attempt to solace his unsatisfied desires with the foul fancies of a mind diseased. And then turn to another picture, drawn by no less a master hand; Dante's love for Beatrice, pure, passionate, reverent, intense; and mark how it leads him onward and upward evermore; on past the awful sight of sin and its abhorrence; on through the discipline of penitential pain; on to the vision of the uncreated loveliness, there, among the purified, to worship face to face.

We see the drift of our own tendencies more clearly by looking at their issues in this way "writ large," their reflection in the mirror of genius. And every heart that has ever loved must know, either in great or small degree, the truthfulness to nature of one or other of these pictures. To love is to be lifted or degraded by our love, in proportion as we repudiate or welcome the law of sacrifice. The forms which that sacrifice may take are infinite, but the fact of it needs no proof. Each of us feels it the moment he looks his own experience in the face, and its essence is always the same. It is the control of the lower impulse by the higher, the sense by the spirit, the body by the soul; the gradual surrender of all self-seeking interests, in order to the welfare of the being whom we love. And although at times the sense of effort melts under the fire of feeling, and self-sacrifice becomes a joy, yet it is only possible through the exercise of will.

Love, then, as we know it, is a relation between persons, founded on desire, tending to self-sacrifice, needing for its true development the guidance of the will. And further, it is never stationary. It withers unless it grows, and in growing gathers purity, intensity, perfection. This is the faculty which we are bidden to enlist wholly in God's service: "Thou shalt love the Lord thy God with all thy heart." How is this to be done? Different forms of personal beauty, different graces of mind or character, wake the love of different men. But once let a man be confronted by the congenial character, the appropriate grace, and nature does the rest. So with the love of God. He attracts us through many avenues. Our part is to direct our mental vision by the will; and then

> We needs must love the highest when we see it.

But it is in this direction of our vision that we fail. Our eyes are feeble, and we cannot bear the light. "He left not Himself without witness," but we interpret it amiss.

The simplest of all witnesses is our natural desire for God. "All men yearn for the gods," said the Greek, "My soul is athirst for God," said the Hebrew poet. In spite of such utterances, a century ago philosophers could still maintain that religion was artificial. But in the light of our larger knowledge this is no longer possible. For however far we look back over India, or Babylon, or Egypt, or abroad over the savage inmates of the islands of the sea, the religious instinct is there; not merely a fear, or a sense of infinitude, but a yearning, a desire, the beginning of a love. So universally is it found to be part of our primitive endowment, that zoologists have proposed, for their special purpose, to classify mankind as "the religious animal." This desire is the foundation of all our love. Our capacity for loving God and our capacity for loving man are one and the selfsame thing. Or to put it otherwise, we have an infinite capacity for loving, which points to an Infinite Being as its only final object. But what do we mean by an Infinite Being? not one who excludes, but who includes all else that is lovely in Himself, as infinite space includes all finite spaces; so that in loving whatsoever things are lovely here on earth among our fellow-men, we are using, training, developing, expanding the same faculty which leads in the end to our loving God. This is the meaning of that intimate blending of divine with human love which we find throughout St. John. "If we love one another, God dwelleth in us, and His love is perfected in us." Our own experience will prove this, if we interpret it aright. Limit your love exclusively to any finite thing or person, and what is the result, and why? Sooner or later it will begin to flag; it will fail; it will become disgust; and that because you have thought to limit what never can be limited. But love one person truly—child, wife, husband, brother, friend— and see where your love, untrammelled, will lead you in the end: not away from them, but through them, desire outsoaring opportunity, into wider and wider worlds of sympathy in feeling and in deed; and all this because it is by its very nature limitless.

We are all of us endowed, then, with an emotional capacity, whose final cause is the love of God. And every phase of human emotion should be, and may be if we will, a stage in the training of this faculty for its destined end and goal.

There is, for instance, the love of nature—of the beauty of earth and sea and sky, and of all the various life with which they teem. It appeals to men unequally, but the class of minds which it affects was never, perhaps, larger or more susceptible than now. Our habits of travel, our physical science, our landscape art, have all conspired to invest the aspect of the natural world with an unique influence on modern life. And how is that influence used? The materialist often uses it to lull to sleep those inconvenient instincts which his creed can find no place for, and yet cannot suppress—

> Some vague emotion of delight
> In gazing up an Alpine height,
> Some yearning toward the lamps of night.

He feels all this, but can allow it no reality. It is a relief to his pent-up energies to give such feelings scope; but in the end they return unsatisfied, and only leave him more forlorn. The man of æsthetic temper, again, who feels himself endowed with a finer sense of beauty than his fellows, often makes the intensity with which he worships nature stand him in the stead of a religion. But a religion of mere beauty obliterates our moral distinctions, and leads to sentimental apathy, if not corruption, in the end. Contemplate nature, without a bias, and it will teach other things than this. Its loveliness will strengthen and develop your emotions, but in doing so will point them on, with irresistible suggestiveness, to One lovelier than itself. "The heavens declare the glory of God, and the firmament showeth His handiwork" is not only the universal verdict of the Hebrew heart, but of all the greatest interpreters of nature in bygone ages, as well as of those who are not unworthy to be named in their company to-day.

And then there is the love of art. Art selects and rearranges nature, with a view to bring its lessons more intimately home. And it is for us to choose what lessons in our case it shall bring. It might seem superfluous to pause over the broad distinction between the art that lifts to heaven and the art that drags to hell. Conscience is critic enough between the two. It is in the borderland where they mingle and their outlines are confused that our real danger lies. We allow ourselves forms of art which are intrinsically harmless, but which, with our own especial tendencies, are full of deadly harm for us; or we are tempted to erect the law, which our own weakness may make needful, the plucking out of our eye and the cutting off of our hand, into a standard for all others, and so make our brother to offend. Our duty is to use all art that will kindle our emotions nobly, but sternly to forego, even in what may seem the neutral region of amusement, all that is insidiously poisonous to us, and yet may innocently brighten and help the lives of other men. This fact needs insisting on; for artistic influences elude observation, and we are hardly aware of how profoundly painting, music, drama, poetry, and the immense literature of fiction mould and modify for good or evil every fibre of our modern life.

Again, there is the love of humanity, the most universal of all schools of love.

In the early dawn of affection we idealise our dear ones with an instinctive insight that is in truth prophetic of what they may one day be. But here and now they are finite beings—weak, sinful, incomplete; and the tender tones of the morning mist must vanish in the midday sun. Differences of taste and temper, inadequacies, imperfections, cannot but disclose themselves, as time goes on. And then, if our first love was, after all, but a refined selfishness, or an animal affection gracefully disguised, the result is disappointment, antipathy, disgust, embittered life, or open shame; and the thing that seemed once so lovely comes to be thought a mere delusion, a marsh fire born only to lead its followers astray. But if our love be true, we shall learn to efface our selfishness in helping other lives to overcome their insufficiencies; and every sacrifice this costs us will deepen our power of sympathy; we shall feel not only for the grace and beauty, but for all the pathetic frailty of the struggling human soul; and as we learn, by loving more profoundly, the limitless nature of our love, we shall see that its only adequate satisfaction is in God—

Nor man nor nature satisfies whom God alone created.

These are the two paths along which human affection leads. And there is no other. We are apt to look lightly on love as on a pleasant dream of youth from which we must sooner or later awake to the work of life. But it is no dream; it is a heavenly vision at the parting of the ways; a vision of the great reality that shall outlast earth, and still endure, when prophecies have ceased and when knowledge has vanished away. Think, before you reject the vision, of St. Paul's terrible portrait of those who changed "the truth of God into a lie, and worshipped and served the creature more than the Creator" —a portrait as awfully true to the life of modern London as of ancient Rome. And think also of those other words of the great Apostle of love: "He that dwelleth in love, dwelleth in God, and God in him."

There is one more school of affection; but we can only learn its lessons if we come to it, at least in some degree, prepared; for it is the school of bereavement. To the idolater of nature, or of art, or of humanity, we know what the shattering of his idol means; hopeless, helpless, impotent despair; weeping and wailing and gnashing of teeth. And yet it was not meant to be, it never need be, so. If once we have risen to realise that what we love on earth can have derived its loveliness from no other source than God, bereavement, however bitter, is full of earnest meaning. We cannot help being bowed down by it; we cannot check our agonised questionings; for the moment the heart seems dead. But when the fury of the storm is over, we can recognise its blessings. There will be a thousand consolations, it may chance, of our sorrow; but with these we are not now concerned. Our concern is with the fact that bereavement reveals to us new and mysterious vistas in the life of love. All along we have seen that sacrifice of one kind or other must be present. But bereavement shows us how intensely real that sacrifice must be. All else seems to vanish before it; and the very name of *love* acquires an awfulness which makes its light misuse seem blasphemy. Even our Lord could say to His disciples, "It is expedient for you that I go away," and that expediency throws light upon every lesser human parting. It is the needful way by which our love must be strengthened, spiritualised, uplifted, glorified. And it is a way which we must enter each one by himself alone. Its solitude is the source of all its fruitfulness. It leads us into the wilderness, there to be taught by God; and in that teaching all our earlier, lighter lessons merge and end.

Such are the common means by which we may learn to fulfil the commandment "Thou shalt love the Lord thy God with all thy heart." The genius can dispense with the ordinary methods of education; and so too can the saint; but for most of us it is otherwise. The things that lie around us, the stuff that life is made of, the field of our daily exercise—nature, art, society, marriage, friendship, partings, death,—these are the appointed channels that should guide the heart to God. Our mistake is to think such things indifferent, as if there were a neutral region, neither good nor ill. Nothing is indifferent, except to our blindness. Every object of human interest lifts us up or drags us down. And though self-discipline may call us away from one or another of the things of earth, Christian asceticism is wholly independent of the false philosophy, which teaches that God is to be loved by turning our back upon His creatures, as if He were the Emptiness and not the Fulness which filleth all in all.

## IV

# THE SERVICE OF THE MIND

"Thou shalt love the Lord thy God . . . with all thy mind."
ST. MATT. xxii. 37.

THE mind is the faculty which distinguishes us as men. Through whatever stages of development our history may have passed, it is from the moment of our possessing a self-conscious mind that all our after faculties ceased to be merely animal, and became distinctively human. Our service of God, therefore, must be a reasonable service. Its initial act is "to believe that He is, and that He is a rewarder of them that diligently seek Him," and this is an act of mind. Its goal is mental intuition, "to know the love . . . which passeth knowledge," "to know as we are known."

Now, the first difficulty that meets us, in attempting to serve God with our mind, is the weakness of our will to do so. "He that willeth to do . . . shall know" is the condition of such service, as of all other intellectual success. But when we attempt to put this precept into practice we soon find that our will does not act as we could wish. It is diseased, more deeply diseased than we are at all aware, and our only wisdom is to face the fact. It is easy enough to make light of the Scriptural account of the fall of man. But the fact itself is not so easily got rid of; for its evidence is everywhere, within us and around us. We have only to look back over our own history, our faded ideals, our frequent failures, our daily falsehood to our better self—the secret thoughts, and words, and deeds that we cannot recall without a flush of shame—in order to feel that the governing principle within us is diseased. And when in the light of this self-knowledge we look round upon the outer world we see everywhere "writ large" the consequences of the self-same weakness that we feel within; broken hearts, ruined families, the countless victims of defrauded trust or of betrayed affection, the shameful sights of the city street, the suicide of the gambler, the despair of the condemned cell. Trace these things backwards and you will find that they seldomer spring from deliberate malice than from the accumulated complications due to impotence of *will*. Tito Melema is the average man. "To will is present with me, but how to perform that which is good I find not." Such is the universal experience of our race; as familiar to the saint as to the sinner, to the heathen philosopher as to the Christian apostle; and it is only a statement of the fact that we have a fallen, and ever-falling *will*. There is no need to darken the picture, as theological sectarians have often done; but there is great need to have it oftener in mind than is our wont.

Nor is this all. There are tendencies of the age in which we live exceptionally calculated to destroy our strength of will. It is an age of luxury in the widest extension of the term. In old days that word was used to signify exclusively the sins of the flesh; and they have an unique effect, of which their victims are too often unaware, in paralysing energy of will. But, in the larger sense of the word, we live in a luxurious atmosphere, which is none the less dangerous for being produced by causes, many of which in themselves are good. We have exchanged the jolting road for a life that runs smoothly upon rails. We expect our senses to be treated softly. We aim at a maximum of ease. Life in our schools is passed more delicately; suffering is reduced by the anæsthetic appliances of science; war is mitigated; penal laws are more humane; a thousand alleviations lessen the rubs and jars of life. But vastly as this picture may compare to advantage with those of many a bygone age, there is one unspeakably serious shadow on it all. Its whole tendency is fatal to a robust development of will. The influence of such a tendency may seem unimportant from its subtlety. Not so. It is the action of subtle influences, impalpable, yet omnipresent as the air we breathe, that make or mar the character of average mankind. It was not against obvious sins that our Lord cautioned His disciples so much as against the deceitful leaven that permeates respectable society.

Again, we live in an age of unparalleled distraction. Secular thinkers are as anxiously aware of it as spiritual teachers, for it is as hostile to all serious culture as to depth of religious life. Civic centralisation, with its attendant rush and hurry, the intensified struggle for existence, the craving of the jaded nerves to be passively amused, the rush of literature that dazzles the eye and is gone without entering the mind—all these, inevitable elements as they have become of modern life, distract, bewilder, dissipate the powers of the will. It is among far other scenes than these that heroic wills are nurtured and high purposes confirmed. It is in the desert, in the mountain solitude, in the secret chamber, on the lonely shore—and there not till the whirlwind and the storm have passed away—that saints and prophets and patriots have learned to set their faces as a flint. "Come ye apart into a desert place, and rest awhile" is a call which we, too, need as much as did the disciples long ago, for there are still "many coming and going." Detachment of one kind or another from the distractions of our daily life, intervals of solitude with our conscience and our God, are as needful now as ever, if we would "possess our souls" and cultivate our energy of will.

All this should be remembered when we are bidden to love God with all our minds. For to direct our mind aright, and to sustain it in the right direction, requires a continuous operation of will that can never be maintained without watchful, prayerful discipline.

We need only consider the conditions of modern intellectual life to see how true this is. Literature is ever increasing, while leisure decreases daily. We have no time to think things out, and yet are expected to have our opinions; and by consequence we must skim over the results of thought without pausing on their methods of attainment. The volume gives place to the more compendious essay, the essay to the paragraph, the paragraph to the latest catchword of criticism or of science; and intelligent appreciation takes the place of intellectual effort. The natural effect of this is a superficial acquaintance with many subjects, incompatible with the thorough understanding of any one. And yet it is under conditions such as these that we daily hear discussed around us, without apparent sense of incongruity, all the fundamental problems of religion and philosophy.

We have need, then, in the present age, to watch our motives very closely when we engage in conversation or discussion of the things of God. "For the holy spirit of discipline will flee deceit, and remove from thoughts that are without understanding, and will not abide when unrighteousness cometh in." It is possible, for instance, to adopt new views prematurely, from reasons which, if we examine them honestly, will turn out to be disguised vanity—the desire to appear clever, or the fear to be thought behind the age. And Agnosticism is often professed by those who have no right whatever to the name; not as the sad attitude of solemnly suspended judgment, after evidence duly weighed, but as a creditable synonym for the older word Indifferentism—the state of mind which views religion as a thing comparatively unimportant, and which may safely be deferred to that more convenient season which, in truth, it is often hoped may never come. And even if conscience acquits us of all these kinds of unreality, we may still be in danger of thinking that novelty is a criterion of truth. Time was when men needed warning that the views of theologians on questions of science or philosophy which fell outside their province, were at least of no more authority than those of other men. And now the wheel has come full circle, and we need similar warning in a different direction. The necessity for our accepting ready-made thoughts at second hand has again given exaggerated importance to authority, the authority of the expert student who furnishes us with his results. Knowledge, as it increases, is more elaborately specialised, and the sphere of each special student—the only sphere in which he is an authority—tends therefore, of necessity, to grow proportionately small. Yet in practice this is forgotten, and the man who has made himself a name in any department is accepted, however sincerely he may disclaim the dubious honour, as an authority upon things wholly beyond his province and his ken. This is a serious danger to all true culture, but nowhere more than in theology. And we must bear this fact in mind. "Cuique in suâ arte credendum est." If we must think upon authority, it should always be the authority appropriate to the case. To interpret new discoveries we of course go to new thinkers, and many of these discoveries touch the fringes of our religion, and may involve their re-arrangement. But upon questions that are as old as history, and facts that were more familiar to St. John and to St. Paul, to St. Clement of Alexandria and St. Augustine, than to ourselves, we must turn away from the modern specialist to the masters of the spiritual life. There are many difficulties in the way, therefore, of our growth in religious knowledge; and in meeting them and fighting them, as life goes on, we shall gradually learn to see how profound a moral discipline is involved in the commandment to love God with all our *mind*.

But the commandment applies no less to minds that are over-diffident than to those that are overweening. There is such a thing as cowardice as well as pride of intellect. And the fact that there is a way in which the wayfaring man and the fool shall not err, and that St. Paul speaks in a certain context of the foolishness of preaching, are no excuse for burying our mental talent in a napkin. The "credo quia absurdum" of the fiery African is a less safe motto than the "credo ut intelligam" of the far profounder Anselm. The religious life cannot but be a life of progress. We love our friends the more as we *know* them better; and it must be the same with the love of God. The very nature, indeed, of knowledge is to desire its own increase; and to know God at all, in any real sense, must make us desire fuller knowledge. Moreover, we must remember that none of us liveth to himself; and if we would help our brother-men to-day, it will often have to be by sympathy with their intellectual needs. But timid believers are apt to forget all this, and think and speak as if the religious conceptions of their childhood were final. They are panic-stricken at any call to reconstruct or modify even the most external of their theological defences. When men of science tell them that the antiquity of our race is greater and its origin other than was once supposed, or when Biblical critics bid them qualify their favourite views of Scripture, or when comparative mythologists suggest that many of the ideas that were once supposed to be unique endowments of a chosen people may be part of the primitive property of the entire human race,—they feel their hold upon religion loosened. But if it is so, that hold can never really have been secure. For all these things may be true without touching the essence of the faith; and if true they come from above, from the Father of lights, and their discovery is due to the working of the eternal wisdom in the world. You may suspend your judgment as long as they are unproven; but you must be ready to accept them, should the evidence require it, at whatever cost of tender memories or cherished modes of thought. For the mind has its sacrifices as well as the heart and the will. The ardent mind, as we have seen, must learn to put on humility. But the fearful mind will equally need a discipline in courage. The command to leave father and mother has many applications, and among them it includes the loneliness of the life of independent thought. But with the sacrifice comes also its reward. Your faith will have exchanged its worn-out garments for an ampler, richer robe. New lights will break in upon you; larger notions of God's character; deeper insight into His providence and dealings with the world. While the very impunity with which the faith can change its vesture with the changing ages will but bring its central changelessness into more complete relief.

To resume, then, we have minds and are

bidden to use them in God's service; and in doing so we are beset by one or other of two temptations, which are only specious forms of the old sins of pride and sloth. Both must be resisted, and that resistance will involve nothing less than an earnest, watchful, prayerful exercise of *will*.

Such service is an essential part of our personal religion as well as of our helpfulness to our fellow-men. But there is one further appeal to our mental energies, the mute appeal for teaching of the generations yet unborn. Secularists are eager in the service of posterity. Atheists look forward to a subjective immortality in the recognition by after ages of the work that they have done for men. Shall Christians be indifferent to the future fate of those whom they hope one day to welcome in the world beyond the grave? Had the Christians who have gone before us been so, what were our condition now? St. Paul and St. John, with all their inspiration, were men like ourselves. And yet they never shrank from the intellectual labour of linking the old order of religion to the new. And after them theologians, teachers, doctors, prophets, in unbroken line handed on their sacred message, enforcing, explaining, amplifying, modifying, re-arranging to meet the fresh requirements of each succeeding age. The " massive grouping " of modern ignorance passes them over with a sneer, in its collective condemnation of " the fathers " or " the schoolmen." But the student knows their freedom of inquiry, their conflict with weariness, their intellectual courage, persevering under difficulties far more acute than ours, and recognises in their austerity that note of discipline which must always mark the mind that is wholly bent on serving God.

And then there are the Christian artists, who guided back to holy service those instincts which the earlier world had educated only to misuse; the builders whose works still witness that they "dreamed not of a perishable home"; the painters who have brought more near to us than any written word could do the sorrows of our Master, the realities of judgment, the pathetic power of sanctity that underlies our common life; the poets, known or nameless, that have enriched the poor with hymnody, or filled the mind with images of all that is lovely and of good report; the musicians who lift life upward, in its intervals of pause or prayer, to listen to the echoes of the song before the throne.

We have entered into the fruit of these men's labours; let us take heed that those who come after us be able to enter into ours.

## V

# THE SERVICE OF THE SOUL

"Thou shalt love the Lord thy God . . . with all thy soul."
ST. MATT. xxii. 37.

IN discussing the action of our several faculties, we are obliged to separate them in thought more completely than they ever are separated in fact. In real life the will and the mind and the emotions intertwine and intermingle, and tinge and colour one another in a way that defies analysis. And the reason of this is, that they are only the different modes in which our one central personality acts. Behind them all and their various workings there is that unity which makes us what we are, and which is called by various names—our personality, our soul, our spirit, our self. It is usually called in religious language the soul, in philosophy, the spirit; but both words are

Biblical. "Thou shalt love the Lord thy God . . . with all thy soul." "God is a Spirit: and they that worship Him must worship Him in spirit." This principle is in fact the source, and centre, and necessary condition of our religious life. But before thinking of its operation we must be clear about its nature. For its very existence has been controverted. Men have attempted to resolve the "self" within us into a mere series of impressions, with no separate identity of its own. But any one who has ever been sufficiently influenced by this ingenious *tour de force* to think the question worth examining, knows that the desperate expedients to which Hume and his followers have been driven, reduce their position at last to an absurdity. The simple fact that we can remember and compare the impressions of to-day and yesterday, and still feel keen remorse for our deeds of long ago, is evidence of a something permanent within us, which time and its passing impressions cannot change. It is, indeed, this permanent persistence that has made the doubt seem plausible, for we are apt to overlook what is always present, as, for instance, a continuous sound. But the moment we turn our attention inward, we are immediately conscious, and every language in every age bears witness to the fact, that we possess a persistent personality or self, mysteriously mingling with and yet no less strangely independent of our bodily organism, and which we therefore call spiritual. We cannot define it, except by negative terms, any more than we can define God except by negatives, as Infinite or Incomprehensible; but this does not affect our certitude of its reality. We cannot define it, because in truth we can never place ourselves outside it, for it is our very self. For convenience we call it immaterial, but in doing so we must remember that we know absolutely nothing of what matter really is; and it is safer, therefore, to say that spirit transcends all modes of matter which are known to us; a phrase to which analogy may help us to give meaning. Vitality, for instance, the principle of life, transcends the mechanical and chemical forces with which the human organism is stored. It gathers them up into itself, uses, and in using them raises them to a higher power, and endows them with new capacities, which no knowledge of the lower forces, as they are by themselves, could have predicted or can explain. Or, again, the mind transcends the senses. It receives and uses their reports; but in doing so extends, corrects, multiplies, connects them, lifts them into a wider, larger plain. And analogously we are conscious that our spirit gathers into one all the lesser faculties and functions of our complex being, transmuting them with its own alchemy, investing them with unknown potencies, bearing them aloft into a region they could never reach alone. In this sense the spirit may be said to transcend the body, as rising above and yet including it. Common language views the soul as contained in the body; but in reality it contains the body in its own vaster mode of being; or at the most it is only contained as the light is contained within the lamp, from which it radiates afar into space.

It is necessary to dwell upon this fact, that we are naturally and essentially spiritual beings; because when once clearly understood it orientates us, gives us our true direction, shows us the real meaning of our daily experience of the unrest of sin and the peace of holiness. We are all of us familiar, in our own history or that of others, with those strange cross purposes of the world, which Dante illustrates by the instance that we so often insist on arming the born writer with a sword, and confining the born soldier to the pen. And the same thing is the key to all our moral discord. We are spiritual beings, and the sinful, the self-indulgent, the self-regarding man, is simply out of his true context. He is counterworking his destiny. He is trying to satisfy with the uncongenial pursuits and interests of earth a nature whose true home and sphere of exercise is otherwhere. Thence the unrest, the aimless changefulness, the disappointment, the bitterness, at last the despair, the sorrow of the world that worketh death. And thence also " the peace, which passeth all understanding," of the saint. The way is rough and long, the landscape dreary, the storms frequent, the shelter poor, the night coming; but the goal is the spiritual city, his Father, his friends, his home. We whom he passes on the road, or who pause awhile at the same inn with him, can tell from his mien and speech that he is a stranger seeking a country, his own country, where alone his rank and lineage are known.

For to know that we are spirits is to know that our home is the spiritual world. And what do we know of the spiritual world? We may assist ourselves to realise it by earthly images. Daniel and Ezekiel pictured it in forms borrowed from the walls of Babylon. St. John pictured it under the imagery of the Christian altar-service, and Jerusalem the city built foursquare upon the hills. And the fiends of Dante and the angels of Angelico helped to bring it near to the mediæval mind. And it may be pictured to a scientific age under the forms of natural law, so long as we remember that these too are but earthly pictures. Our Lord's parabolic teaching, and St. Paul's illustration of the risen life, are similar modes of picturing the unseen by the seen. But "the things that are seen are temporal; and the things that are unseen are eternal." Imaginative pictures make the objects of our belief more vivid, but the belief must come before the picturing; and the belief in the spiritual world is an act of faith. For faith is the spirit using its own special faculty. It is not weak reasoning, it is strong sight. It does not act independently of evidence, but it interprets the evidence in the light of its own inner experience, to which a thousand subtle coincidences, secret influences, special providences, give a cogency far too deep for words. To the beginner in the religious life it may seem only to afford probability; but to the saint, whether sage or simple, it is a faculty of certitude. He "knows whom he has believed." He "has heard with the hearing of the ear, . . . but now his eye seeth." His "faith is the assurance of things hoped for, the proving of things not seen." He stands in the full daylight and sees things in their true proportions, and no longer distorted by the treacherous mists of earth. No external critic can pass judgment on the reality of faith; but neither can he on any other subject which is beyond his field of experience. All true knowledge can be criticised only from within. And St. Paul is making no exceptional claim for the spiritual life when he says, "The natural man receiveth not the things of the Spirit of God: for they are foolishness unto him; and he cannot know them, because they are spiritually judged. But he that is spiritual judgeth all things, and he himself is judged of no man." The only appeal is to the spiritual expert, if the phrase may be allowed. And who are the spiritual experts? "The glorious company of the Apostles, the goodly fellowship of the Prophets, the noble army of Martyrs, the holy Church throughout all the world," the spirits and souls of the righteous, the holy and humble men of heart. Ask all these by what power they wrought righteousness, and quenched the violence of fire, and out of weakness were made strong, and they will answer, by the reality of their faith.

To love the Lord our God with all our *soul* is to live the spiritual life, the life of faith. And our conceptions of that life may become more real, if we look at some of the points in which it is contrasted with what St. Paul calls the natural life, always remembering the while that "that is not first which is spiritual, but that which is natural, and afterward that which is spiritual." Nature is the basis upon which faith builds, the rough material which the spirit takes up, transforms, transfigures, glorifies.

There is, for example, a *unity* about the spiritual life which is wanting to the natural. For the natural man is one-sided and discordant in his development. One faculty or group of faculties flourishes to the hurt of the rest. And this is the case not merely where the lower nature is in open rebellion, as with the slaves of passion,-or of pride, or of self-will, but in far less suspected regions. For the virtues of average society are departmental. The soldier must be brave, the man of business upright, the statesman able, the judge just. But such professional excellence is not only compatible, but often co-existent with, sometimes purchased at the cost of, tolerated imperfection of many other kinds. Even the man of culture, who might seem an exception, from his power of reflecting sympathetically every phase of life, is the most acutely conscious of the discord between words and deeds, and of the vanity of knowledge bought at the price of unreality. But the spiritual life is the converse of all this. The spirit is not identical with any of our separate faculties of hand or heart or head, but it is the harmonising agency which acts in each and all of them, maintaining their proportion, controlling their divergencies, making manifest throughout the life a central unity of aim. The natural man *does*. His acts outstrip his character, and weaken him. The spiritual man *is*. His character is greater than his acts, and suggests infinite reserves of energy lying ready to be used. We speak of a man *being* possessed or carried away by a thought or a passion. The spiritual man, with no less intensity, yet knows how to possess *himself*.

And from this follows another of his salient attributes—individuality. It is the common lament of the present day that the "individual withers," though "the world is more and more." The whole scale of modern society seems to be too large, its momentum too tremendous, to be capable of influence by other than massive action. While, in the world of thought, "development" is our universal formula, which means that we look upon the variation rather than the fixity of things; the side of them that fades away into past time or distant space, rather than the separate identity which severs them from all things else. Practical necessity and theoretic tendency alike, therefore, contribute to undermine our modern sense of individuality, to an extent which it is easier to lament than to counteract. But the spiritual man has learnt from the very nature of the life he leads to be independent of popular pressure or fashionable fallacy; and however limited his station or opportunities may be, he will always surpass his fellows in individuality of character, preserving his originality of birthright to the end. In the most commonplace surroundings he can never be commonplace.

And again, the same independence gives to the spiritual character a catholicity of interest, a comprehensiveness of sympathy, peculiarly its own. The natural man, immersed in one kind of pleasure, or pursuit, or society, will always underestimate some class of the community, or race of men, or kind of life. But to the eye of the spirit nothing is insignificant, nothing is intrinsically common or unclean. Even his self-denials are only stages of self-development. "Be not drunk with wine ... but be filled with the Spirit." "There is no man that hath left house, or brethren, or sisters, or mother, or father, or children, or lands, for my sake, and for the gospel's sake, but he shall receive a hundredfold now in this time, houses, and brethren, and sisters, and mothers, and children, and lands, with persecutions." "For all things are yours; whether Paul, or Apollos, or Cephas, or the world, or life, or death, or things present, or things to come; all are yours." "How shall He not also with Him freely give us all things?" These and suchlike passages point us plainly to an infinite fulness as the goal of the spiritual life; and in the light of them, the man of faith regards the world with the tender thoughtfulness of an heir, for some great property which will one day be his own.

The reality of the spiritual life, therefore, is proved by the witness of its countless possessors, by the marvellous deeds and sufferings which it has enabled them to do and bear, and by the harmony, the independence, the catholicity of character which are visible in its contact with the world. And it is needful to dwell upon these proofs in the presence and for the sake of a society which, while it habitually ignores them, often pretends to lament their absence. There is evidence enough and to spare, all round us, of the reality of the spiritual life, to arrest and enforce the attention of any sincere inquirer. And all who follow that evidence from inquiry on to practice will learn, by their own experience, the secret of it all.

For the secret of the spiritual life is its communion with the Father of spirits. The primary objects of our separate faculties are the earthly things that lie around us. But the primary object of the spiritual self that lies behind them is God. For "spirit with spirit can meet." To obey Him and through obedience to know Him, to know Him and through knowledge to love Him, to love Him and through loving to become so intimately one with Him that it is no longer we who live but He that liveth in us—that is the truly natural, because predestined, end of man; and from the fulfilment of that destiny come his power and his peace. His power: for if man were merely an animal, however highly organised, lust, and cruelty, and greed, and pride would be, upon the average and for the mass, inevitable. It is only through the inspiring presence of the divine energy, whether consciously experienced or working unawares, that he can hope to resist temptation however terrible, to conquer sin however alluring, to present his body a living sacrifice, holy, acceptable to God. His peace: for however dimly conscious he may be at first of the nature of that power within him, not himself, which makes for righteousness, time will come, if he obeys its guidance, when the veil shall be withdrawn, and assurance shall take the place of hope ; assurance that He who has begun a good work in him will continue .it unto the end, and that his triumph over sin now is an earnest of triumph over death hereafter. For " if the Spirit of Him that raised up Jesus from the dead dwelleth in you, He that raised up Christ Jesus from the dead shall quicken also your mortal bodies through His Spirit that dwelleth in you."

## VI

## GOD'S LOVE THE CAUSE OF OURS

"We love Him, because He first loved us."—1 JOHN iv. 19.

RECIPROCITY is the crown of love. And although it may be absent in one case or another, we cannot use the word "love," except metaphorically, in any field which does not admit of its possible reciprocation. Any injunction to love God, therefore, will sound abstract and unreal, till we remember that its cause and condition is that "He first loved us." God's condescension, not man's aspiration, is the beginning of religious life. It is not we that work, but "He that worketh in us, both to will and to do according to His good pleasure." But true as this is, it is a truth which, at least in the present day, is far too seldom realised.

There have been times when the sense of the Divine oppressed men, and led to superstition. But such times are not ours. The world of the present day believes, but does not tremble. It thinks, and speaks, and acts, and goes about its business as if our race were, for practical purposes, self-centred and alone. Many causes have contributed to this. The psychological character of our philosophy, leading to agnosticism; our overestimate of liberty, with its attendant shadow self-assertion, to the comparative neglect of obedience, humility, reverence and awe; the splendid spectacle of our vast achievements in mechanism and science,— have all tended to reinforce the natural pride of the human heart, not less ready now than of old to say, "I am, and there is none beside me"; and the result is a society which seems to have forgotten God. And we cannot breathe its atmosphere without being tainted by its poison.

It needs, therefore, a very real effort to bear constantly in mind the fact that we are creatures, and that our nearest relation is our

Creator; for however dependent we may be upon our fellow-creatures, we are far more essentially dependent upon Him in whom "we live, and move, and have our being."

If we turn, then, to the Divine share in the development of our faculties, we shall see that what we call our action may be better described as God's attraction, and that we advance in exact proportion as we let ourselves be led by Him. We are the creatures, science tells us, of our environment. Yes; but the reason why we are so is that our true environment is God.

Take the instance of the will. The denial of its freedom is only a parody of the truth that it must be developed by external law. The laws of nature, the laws of society, the laws of conscience, if we obey them, slowly determine our wills towards that uniform course of conduct which constitutes our character. The character of the scientific, the civilised, the moral man is formed by successive acts of more or less difficult obedience to a particular class of laws. And as obedience brings insight, its whole complexion changes, from unwilling acquiescence in an inevitable necessity, to glad co-operation with a principle, the wisdom of which is known. We do not form ourselves, we are conformed to the law; and by every step in that conformity our true freedom is enlarged. And what is this but saying that God, the source of all law, is for ever at work, attracting our wills into harmony with His will, increasing our liberty, and expanding our capacities, in proportion as that harmony grows more complete; teaching us to see, in what once seemed relentless forces, tokens of His truthfulness, His holiness, His love.

The same is the case with our minds. We study a great author, and in doing so, as the phrase goes, make his thoughts our own. But in reality it is he who throws the spell of his personality upon us, and makes our thoughts his; captivating us, carrying us away, binding us to his chariot-wheels, deafened, stunned, overwhelmed, enslaved by the triumph of his genius; while genius in its turn can receive no higher praise than to be regarded as the fruit of inspiration. So with all other mental objects, the course of the stars, the laws of mathematics, chemical properties, mechanical forces,—they are there, they exist before us; we do not create, we only discover them. Our intellect grows with nourishment, but the nourishment must be given from without. Knowledge, therefore, rightly viewed, is the progressive acceptance of revelation; and thence the moral qualities which we see that it involves. The truth, the word, the wisdom, whereby the worlds were made, unfolds itself to the expectant eye, speaks to the awestruck ear, educates, illuminates, leads the awakened spirit onward, in gradual preparation for the vision face to face of Him whom to know is life eternal.

So, too, our power of loving is drawn into activity from without. The tenderness of our mother, our father's protecting pride, the warm-hearted affections of the companions of our youth, bodily beauty, nobleness of life, sanctity of soul,—all these draw the heart out of us, and teach us what it is to love. But who created them all, and endowed them with their loveliness? God, that He might draw us with the cords of a man, with bands of love. And having so created them, why does He withdraw them so soon to Himself, but that He may draw us with them to love them again in Him and Him in them. "We trust they live in Him, and there we find them worthier to be loved."

The love of God for us once realised has a constraining power that compels us to return it with all our heart, and soul, and mind. But such realisation never can be ours till our faculties are duly disciplined. Only the heart that knows what true love is can read the indications of God's love for us aright. Only the mind that is directed upward can teach the heart that heavenly knowledge. Only the will that has learned obedience can give the mind its true direction. We must will in order to know, and know in order to love, before we can consciously enter within the sphere of the divine attraction.

There remains the crowning evidence that He first loved us. He gave Himself for us. The Word was made flesh, and dwelt among us, and became obedient unto death, even the death of the cross. The Incarnation of our Lord Jesus Christ is the supreme appeal to our love, because it is the supreme proof of His. And yet there are many earnest theists in the present day willing enough to trace the signs of a Divine presence in the universe, but inconsistently stopping short of a belief in the Incarnation. For it is an inconsistent stoppage on the part of any real theist, since God, who is conceived of as caring for His creatures, must be supposed to reveal Himself in ways suiting their capacity; and an Incarnation, as many a pre-Christian thinker saw, would be the reasonable culmination of such ways of self-revealing. But despite its inconsistency such theism is largely prevalent, and liable to delude halfhearted Christians of their hope. It must be carefully borne in mind, therefore, that the same rules which are involved in any religious use of our faculties at all, apply with even greater stringency to our understanding of the Incarnation. If our Lord Jesus Christ be God, as He affirmed and we believe, it will follow that

He can only be recognised as such by the spiritual eye. "To write the history of a religion," says a great critic, "you must have believed it once, but you must no longer believe it." He could not have stated with greater precision the condition which at once and for ever disqualifies him for the task. Cultivated criticism may reconstruct the picture of the life of Christ with unexampled vividness, or trace the occurrence in earlier literature of many of His characteristic sayings, or decompose with great acumen the documents that enshrine His history; may do all, in fact, which can be done for any other bygone hero. But from the fundamental question, "What think ye of Christ, whose son is he?" criticism must shrink abashed; for the answer is not revealed by flesh and blood, but by "His Father which is in heaven." Criticism and obedience exclude each other, and to know we must obey. "If any man willeth to do His will, he shall know of the teaching, whether it be of God, or whether I speak from myself." "He that hath my commandments, and keepeth them, he it is that loveth me . . . and I will love him, and will manifest myself unto him. Judas saith unto him, not Iscariot, Lord, how is it that thou wilt manifest thyself unto us, and not unto the world? Jesus answered and said unto him, If a man love me, he will keep my words: and my Father will love him, and we will come unto him, and make our abode with him." The will to obey, therefore, which we have already seen to be the general condition of all spiritual knowledge, is expressly demanded by our Lord for the knowledge of Himself. Put that will into practice; strive to live out, as He lived them to the bitter end, the superhuman precepts of the Sermon on the Mount. Take up your cross daily, and follow the man Christ Jesus, and you will know, at first negatively— by learning the immeasurable gulf between you—and then positively, as one after another of His lineaments stands out, that "truly this man was the Son of God." And when this conviction has once flashed upon you, His life and death will acquire a new significance; for your mind will recognise that, being God, He must have been divinely free, and therefore must have chosen of His own free will to live and die for you; and your heart will assure you that the only motive for that choice must have been love,—the love with which before we were born, or ever our race created, He first loved us.

There is evidence enough of God's love for us in the beauty of the world, the beneficence of nature, and all the joy of human intercourse. It is only when we come to the dark sad side of life that our faith begins to fail. And here the Incarnation takes up the thread of proof, not by removing the problem of the mystery of sorrow from our minds, but by revealing God Himself as willing to bear it with and for us, and so enabling our hearts to feel it the crowning testimony of His love. The soul that has reached this certitude needs no other motive to ensure its obeying the commandment, "Thou shalt love the Lord thy God." But there are many who have not attained it, from fearing to make the initial venture of taking up their cross. With all their disbelief in miracles, they still seek after a sign. A sign, they must remember, cannot produce conviction; for conviction comes by obedience, and by that alone. But a sign may arrest attention, and lead to obedience in the end. And there is a sign which outsoars all other miracles, and only grows more wonderful as the ages pass along, and that is the empire of Jesus Christ over human hearts. He claimed it, and history has justified the claim. No other founders of religions, patriots, martyrs, kings, or saints, have ever claimed it or received it. In all history it is unique. Critics tell us that the sayings of the Sermon on the Mount were not original, and the suffering of Calvary no greater than what other men have borne, and even that the Gospel narratives are in many points inaccurate. But all these things, if granted, only force into stronger relief the wonder of the fact that Jesus Christ crucified, dead, and buried, more than eighteen centuries ago, has inspired in every age, and among wholly diverse nations, in thousands after thousands of sinful and saintly hearts alike, not merely reverence for His memory, or sympathy for His sufferings, or enthusiasm for His cause, but a personal, passionate, living adoration, passing the love of woman; and characterised by a finality, a restfulness, a peace, which finite objects of affection never can afford. That this is so is a fact beyond the reach of controversy, and a fact which defies explanation on any other view than that Jesus Christ is God—the Infinite and therefore adequate Object of human love, the desire of all nations, who alone could say, "I, if I be lifted up, will draw all men unto me."

Thus our various faculties contain within themselves the laws of their own right usage. We may deny or disobey those laws, but are forced if we do so to admit in the end that all things are vanity and vexation of spirit, and that it were better we had never been born. But if we obey them, they will lead us with unerring instinct on to God; and the nearer we approach Him the more fully shall we realise that it is not we who are seeking Him, so much as He that is seeking us; seeking us, because He made us to find our joy in Him alone.

# VII

## INNOCENCE

"Blessed are the pure in heart: for they shall see God."
ST. MATT. v. 8.

IT is a familiar fact that types of character change with the changing ages. One or more forms of excellence, or what is thought to be excellence, stand out from time to time above others, and set the fashion which men consciously imitate or unconsciously reflect. In comparatively simple ages these types are few and marked; but in a complex period like our own they are wont to be more numerous and less defined. Practical problems which at other times have presented themselves singly, seem now, in indiscriminate confusion, to press for solution all at once. And speculative opinions which have risen in succession and superseded one another in the past, are now revived and co-exist among us, as in the bewildering variety of a great museum. We have more objects, aims, ideals, vocations, professions, creeds, among which to choose; and a corresponding multiplicity in the kinds of character which these things go to form. But however many and different these resulting types, they have all one point in common. They are all touched and tinged by the complexity of the conditions to which they owe their birth. The modern man is naturally complex; even the simplest modes of life and thought being now more complicated than would once have been the case. And since men like what they are accustomed to, we have come to value this complexity. It has become a standard of judgment with us, and often an ideal of attainment. In affairs, we admire the man of most varied interests, the most versatile man; and in speculation the man of widest intellectual sympathy with opposite modes of thought; while as a teacher we prefer the critic to the prophet, the man who can best apply our favourite formula, the comparative method, to the man with a single idea, however great, a single aim, however good. Generalisations of this kind may be thought to require qualification, and may in fact do so. But they would hardly seem to be unfair descriptions of the average temper of our day.

Now it is this average condition of an age which, like the temperament of a man, determines the direction of its spiritual dangers. Violent ages, effeminate ages, ignorant ages, present each a special difficulty to the pursuit of the religious life. And so does a complex age which loves its own complexity. It is hostile to that simplicity and purity of heart and mind which constitute what in theological language is called Innocence. It not merely makes the preservation of innocency difficult, for that is a difficulty common to every age, but it dethrones the innocent type of character from its place of solitary eminence, as the standard by which all others must be judged. We admire the imaginary portraits of Galahad or Percival, and are touched by the descriptions of Pompilia, or Colonel Newcome, or Lord Fauntleroy; but we are neither quick to recognise, nor desirous to imitate their rare counterparts in real life. We have framed for ourselves a false ideal, in which width of experience is preferred to depth of insight, extent of action or appreciation to intensity of character.

Yet in sharp and decisive contrast to all this, our Lord puts simplicity of character and innocency of life before either width of thought, or abundance of action, as being the sole root out of which right action and true thought can come. "Jesus called a little child unto Him, and set him in the midst of them, and said, Verily I say unto you, Except ye be converted, and become as little children, ye shall not enter into the kingdom of heaven." And from that day to this the Christian Church has known two conditions, and two only, in her members; innocence, the state of those who, however little they might claim the honour, have kept themselves unspotted from the world; and penitence, the state of all others, whom she bids mourn with a lifelong sorrow for the innocence that they have lost.

It may be especially worth our while, then, to pause upon this thought of "innocence" in the midst of a complicated age. It is obviously a relative term ; for who can tell how oft he offendeth? But still it is plain enough to be easily distinguished, not perhaps by its possessor, but by all who behold it from without ; and the type of character which it denotes is definite. Innocence in its theological sense is not childish, but childlike ; not the negative state of the untempted, but the confirmed habitual state of those who have been brought through the fire, and refined as silver is refined, and tried as gold is tried, and purified and made white. It is the grace of those who have loved God at first sight, and have never fallen away from that first love. Others reach God as the result of the weary negative induction which Augustine has described for all time. But the innocent are those who have been true to the divine ideals, through which in youth the beauty of holiness flashes on the soul ; content to take the evil in the world upon authority, till time has shown them its malignity without imparting its contagion; and therefore able in the end to say, "I have more understanding than my teachers, for Thy testimonies are my study. I am wiser than the aged: because I keep Thy commandments."

Let us consider, then, why innocence is so high a state, and its loss such a remediless woe. First, there is its effect upon the conscience. Conscience with most of us acts irregularly at times, like a compass that is not true; and we are apt to throw the blame of this upon every cause but the right one. There is so much to be said on both sides of a case, there are so many aspects of any given course of conduct, such important qualifications of what at first seems to be right, that, with what we believe to be the best intentions, we are nevertheless perplexed, and quite at a loss to know what we ought to do; and further, as our conduct profoundly and intimately affects our creed, paralysis of the one issues in confusion of the other; our mind is "in wandering mazes lost," and cannot tell what to think or believe. We pity ourselves for this, and talk of the complexity of life and its problems, the peculiarity of our circumstances, the difficulty of our situation; and in all this there may be an element of truth. But there is something behind it all. We have tampered with our conscience in a greater or less degree, and precisely in that degree it has lost its early characteristics of directness and simplicity. Its commands are no longer imperative. The rapidity and clearness of its judgments are gone. The light that is in us has become darkness. We have an evil heart of unbelief. Of course the amount of this degradation is very various, and its process often so gradual that we are almost unaware of it. We resent its imputation as an impertinence, and even carry our self-deceit so far as to blame our Creator for a defect in our nature, which we ourselves have caused. But with the innocent all this is otherwise. The conscience which has been habitually obeyed acts with a precision and a clearness, which even the most complex circumstances cannot overcome. It pierces hypocrisies, sweeps aside sophisms, scorns the compromises of cowardice; sees, feels, judges, acts with a decision which men of the world may scoff at, but before which in the long-run they bow. For such a conscience is an incomparable force, and force in the end must tell. The sinful man who is tongue-tied before the innocence of childhood may attribute the feeling to his own tenderness or power of self-control; but in truth it is the might of innocence which has cast its unearthly spell upon him, and he quails unawares before one whose angel still beholds the face of the Father which is in heaven. But let such innocence continue through maturity to age, and there is no mistaking then the source of the awe which it inspires. We may smile behind its back, depreciate, criticise, caricature it. But no sooner does it look us in the face than we must slink away abashed, beginning at the eldest even unto the last. For we are in the presence of one who can see God.

Again, a moral force is an intellectual force. Any serious analysis of the mind and its operations shows us at once how the colour and complexion and delicate accuracy of intellectual work, depends largely upon the moral character of the worker—his patience, his perseverance, his humility, his fairness, his thoroughness, his energy, his zeal; and therefore upon the sincerity of conscience by which the moral character is guided. But apart from all such qualities, which are as it were imbedded in the intellect, and inseparable from its proper action, there is a direct and special way in which innocency is an intellectual force. As the fields of knowledge open before the mind, especially under such easy conditions as those upon which superficial knowledge is now accessible, the temptations to purposeless excursions of vague curiosity increase. And though curiosity is the parent, it is also the enemy of knowledge, and requires to be held in severe control, or it will soon grow with indulgence to the exhaustion and exclusion of all true intellectual life. It substitutes the semblance for the reality, deceives the ignorant into thinking themselves wise, and ends in that negative omniscience, which from Ecclesiastes to Faust has plunged the unsanctified intellect into ever-deepening despair. This is true of all curiosity; but it is far more darkly and sadly true of those forms of it which, for all their intellectual disguise, are immediately hurtful to the spiritual life. They creep upon us in the name of culture, and humanism, and a liberal acquaintance with all that men have thought or done; and the motto "nihil humani alienum" is the fair pretext under which we sully the imagination, and debase the heart, and dissipate the powers of the soul. Now the intuition of innocence sees through all this. No man or woman can preserve that priceless jewel who has not fought the temptation to curiosity in one or more of its many forms, and known something of the bitter struggle to bring every thought into captivity to Christ; for this is the very essence of the warfare by which innocence is strengthened and matured. Consequently, while the curious have weakened and degraded their faculties for using the experience they have gained, the innocent possess an imagination which is their servant and not their master, a memory that is a storehouse of knowledge, not a haunted chamber of remorse, a reason that has not been paralysed by straining at impossible tasks, a will that has not lost the power of issuing in action, pure affections that instinctively tend to guide the mind aright ; and theirs, and theirs alone, in the end is the vision of the truth that shall make free. "For into a malicious soul wisdom shall not enter, nor dwell in the body that is subject unto sin. For the holy spirit of discipline will flee deceit, and remove from thoughts that are without understanding, and will not abide when unrighteousness cometh in." " For wisdom is a loving spirit."

Again, a conscience that acts truly, and a mind that is in control, naturally intensify the whole force of a character. For much of the available energy of most men has to be spent in undoing the results, making up for the misuse, unlearning the mistakes, unravelling the tangled threads of their own past time and opportunities—much of their energy, because it is infinitely harder to erase than to impress. "Teach me," bitterly exclaimed Themistocles to the man who offered to improve his memory, "teach me to forget." But the innocent in proportion to their innocence are spared this labour. No phantom fires mislead them, born of the miasma of past sins. No secret shame, no agony of evil, no weary sense of hopelessness, have to be met and overcome at each fresh forward step. The whole energy of their character is at once available for use. The result of this may not always indeed be visible at once. The man of more complex, even if more distorted development, may for a while appear to possess wider sympathies, or superior strength. But his sympathy will be deficient in moral tone, and apt, therefore, to enervate its object; or his strength will be too stern and have something repulsive about it; whereas the sympathy of the innocent has the strength of inward self-possession, while their strength is veiled with grace. And in time this difference will out. Both men may do good work, but that of the innocent will be more perfect. For the man who feels that his sympathy with others may be affected by the bias of his own past sins, will not only distrust himself, but beget a like distrust in the recipients of his comfort, or his charity, or his help. But the man who starts from a centre of habitual self-control, though his field of experience may at first be narrow, and the compass of his sympathy less complete, has a sureness of touch which attracts the confidence of all within its range, while its range, as the years accumulate, will indefinitely increase. And again, the man whose life is a long battle with his past, will carry too much of the harshness of conflict into regions where it is misplaced, whereas the strength, which is a development, not a reaction from all that has gone before, will be more harmonious, less liable to err, and far more effective in the end. Christian life would have lost much had Augustine's earlier years been different; but a great school of Christian theology would have gained in tenderness and truth; and a hideous heresy on the condition of childhood might perhaps never have been known.

Again, the strength of innocence, being of this harmonious kind, issues in an unique attractiveness. It is in fact as inseparable from the beauty of holiness as are the masses of the mountains from their ethereal glory, or the mighty muscles of the wild animals from their sinuous agility and grace. Simplicity and purity, indeed, fascinate us when they are only natural virtues, untried as yet in the fire, and therefore unconfirmed. But when the same graces exist in those over whom all the waves and storms of life have passed, they exercise a power over us, which it is impossible to analyse; and which the outer world, while wondering, attributes to all sources but the true one, the white-heat of an innocent life. The beauty of an harmoniously developed nature, the insight that a pure conscience gives, intellectual vigour, moral integrity, are all blended in the result. But none of these taken separately, nor even altogether, will account for the peculiar effluence which radiates from innocent souls. They are ministers of the spirit, invested with something of His awful power, of the refiner's fire, and the two-edged sword. Their presence in a company elevates and dignifies its tone; wins others to silent sympathy with all that is lovely and of good report; flashes arrowy lightnings of regret and shame into the dark places of sinful hearts. They are, in an especial sense, the generation of God's children. They go on their way brightening every scene through which they pass; lights of the world, salt of the earth, followers of the Lamb; living extensions of the Incarnation, living temples of the Holy Ghost; their flesh a sacrament, their voice a sermon, their glance a revelation of the spiritual world.

Now we cannot aim at a virtue for any secondary object; because it will give us clearness of judgment, or intellectual success, or force of character, or moral attractiveness; but these things, as Austin shows of utility, may indicate what they do not constitute. And what they indicate in this case is that innocence is the true condition of human excellence, the condition under which man is most truly man; and that because it is the condition in which, and in which alone, he is in his true relation to God. Indeed the difficulty of speaking about it adequately or worthily arises from this very fact. Innocence is what it is, because it possesses the benediction of the pure in heart.

I

It sees God in a way and a degree which is otherwise impossible; and therefore, like all high mystic experience, it refuses to be translated into the imperfect language of our lower world. We can summarise a few of the external notes by which its presence may be known, but its inner secret is its own and God's. And this may suggest a further reason for dwelling upon the grace of innocence in the present day. Modern cultivation has involved a larger class than heretofore in a superficial acquaintance with philosophy. Philosophy is popularised, as far as that is possible, with the consequence that it has come to be viewed as a branch of study that may be pursued or declined at will, rather than as the ultimate analysis and explanation of life. But in order to make this possible it is divorced from theology; a divorce which is of course inconceivable to the philosophic mind, but which crept into the world a few centuries ago, partly from unworthy, partly from worthy though mistaken motives; and has been perpetuated since, sometimes from reverence, sometimes from cowardice, sometimes from sheer stupidity and confusion of mind. With the general results of this strange perversion of truth we are not now concerned; but one of its departmental consequences is that moral philosophy is often treated without reference to God. The effect of this upon a religious mind is that moral philosophy seems meaningless; an ingenious exercise of the understanding, but purely abstract and apart from the real conduct of daily life, with all its trials and temptations and awful issues. But a far worse evil is the alternative assumption that we can be moral without being religious; without, that is, any direct reference of our conduct to our religious views. The practical impossibility of this may be seen even in the extreme case of the Agnostic. His religious views may be chiefly negative, but they contain a positive kernel, and in proportion as he is in earnest, his moral conduct will be causally connected with that positive element, or implication of his creed. And with every increase in the definition of our creed, its separation from our conduct becomes more impossible, till for the Christian the love of God is the formal cause, the constitutive essence of his whole morality; virtues ranking in accordance with the degree of that love which they involve and exhibit. Now the bearing of all this upon our subject is obvious. Innocence is what it is in virtue of being the state of closest union with God, and apart from the thought of that union is negative, colourless, incomplete. Consequently, in a society which has become familiar with the idea that morality is independent of religion, innocence will easily sink into a subordinate position, as one among many graces of character, but not the standard type and source of all. And thus the spiritual danger to which, as we have already seen, a complex age is always liable, will be further increased by the unsound method in which our moral philosophy is often taught, or at least regarded. But to what purpose, it may be asked, is this talk of innocence? Who among us has kept his senses in such complete control, and his mind in such disciplined obedience, as to be worthy of that high name? Is it not an abstract ideal which, at least in the present day, cannot be realised, whatever may have been the case in more ascetic and less practical ages? No; there are still men and women going about amongst us whose conversation is in heaven, and who have kept themselves unspotted from the world. And the earlier we learn to look for them, and to live by their example, the nearer we may one day be to their goal. For after all there are degrees of innocence. We all in our measure start with its possession, and are painfully conscious of the first stages of its loss. Then comes a crisis. Shall we acquiesce in our degradation, and turn for comfort to the morbid experience, with all its unreal pathos, of friends or writers who have gone before us down the pathway of decline? Or shall we look facts in the face, and call things by their true names, and use the methods of recovery which the saints in every age have endorsed with their authority, and enforced by their example—penitence, discipline, and prayer? Penitence can withdraw the veil of sin from between self and God. Discipline, within the limits dictated by our Lord Himself—" If thy right eye cause thee to offend, pluck it out "—will restore the body and the mind alike to due condition of obedient service. Prayer reunites the soul to Him who is of too pure eyes to behold iniquity. These are plain and rugged methods, and in point of picturesqueness far inferior to the romance and glamour that decorate the avenues of sin. But their issue is clearness of conscience, strength of intellect, force of will, beauty—the unearthly beauty of one whose eye is on the uncreated loveliness, and who "grows like what he beholds"; the restoration, at least in a measure, of that innocence of character which was beginning to totter to its fall.

But the process of degradation may have gone farther and lasted longer, till we are very far removed from the high hopes that once were ours. Then more than ever, when we are tempted to depreciate, if not cynically to disbelieve, in innocence, its contemplation, however painful, will be our chiefest need. For without it we have no standard of penitence, no measure of the height whence we have fallen ; and indeed the word repentance will have no meaning for our ears. Yet the decay of penitence is in a way more disastrous, because it covers a wider field even than the decay of innocence itself. The two are causally connected, and much of the perplexity and doubt and insincerity and aimlessness and weariness of men is due to the fact that, from ignoring their loss of the life of innocence, they fail to realise in any true degree their call to the life of repentance, its power of restoration, its energy, its peace. It is this which gives eternal significance to the great poem of Dante, and should make us welcome its increasing influence with hope—its exhibition of the way by which in the soul of a true man the sight of innocence is the spur of penitence.

"Blessed," indeed, "are the pure in heart: for they shall see God." But "blessed" also "are they that mourn"—mourn bitterly for the lost innocence which can never again be theirs —"for they shall be comforted."

# VIII

## VOCATION

"Then Samuel answered, Speak; for Thy servant heareth."
1 SAM. iii. 10.

THE call of Samuel is an extreme and vivid instance of a truth of which the Bible is full; the truth that we are all called of God to our several places and occasions of action or of passion, of working or of waiting in the world; in a word, that we all have a vocation. We hardly need the Bible to tell us this, for it is one of the simplest truths of natural religion. The evidences of providential purpose in the world have been criticised in every age, and never more so than in our own. But they have proved too strong to be upset by criticism, and still remain as they have ever been, among our most necessary forms of thought. And as man is the crown and climax of the visible creation, we naturally expect the purpose which is so abundantly visible elsewhere, to obtain also in the life of man. He too must have a purpose, and to be created for a purpose is, in the case of a free being, to be called to its fulfilment. Thus the vocation of man is a corollary from the design in the world, and may fairly, therefore, be called a part of our natural religion. The New Testament takes up and intensifies this thought; addressing Christians as "the called of Jesus Christ," "called to be saints," "called according to God's purpose," "called unto the fellowship of His Son Jesus Christ our Lord," "called out of the darkness," "called to liberty," "called to eternal life," "called to inherit a blessing," "called to glory and virtue," and bidding us "walk worthy of the vocation wherewith we are called."

Now it hardly needs saying that, for all its naturalness and scriptural authority, we are too apt to forget this thought; and by forgetting it to lose its warning, its encouragement, its guidance—the energy, the hope, the comfort, the success that it should bring.

> What is the course of the life
> Of mortal men on the earth ?—
> Most men eddy about
> Here and there—eat and drink,
> Chatter and love and hate,
> Gather and squander, are raised
> Aloft, are hurled in the dust,
> Striving blindly, achieving
> Nothing ; and then they die—
> Perish, and no one asks
> Who or what they have been,
> More than he asks what waves,
> In the moonlit solitudes mild
> Of the midmost Ocean, have swelled,
> Foam'd for a moment, and gone.

That is no untrue picture of the spectacle of life: and yet these men, whose career the poet likens to "an eddy of purposeless dust," have none the less been called one by one to glory and to virtue, and shall be called again from the rising up of the sun unto the going down thereof, that God may judge His people.

Let us consider the details of the call of

Samuel to his life's work. Circumstances, as we say, but circumstances of which a mother's prayer was part, determine the sphere in which that work is to be done. "The child did minister unto the Lord before Eli the priest." Then comes the Divine voice calling him by name; calling him out of the many possibilities of an office which he shared with such men as Eli's sons, to his own especial and high prophetic destiny. The true nature of that call, misunderstood by him at first, is interpreted by the experienced insight of the aged Eli. "Eli perceived that the Lord had called him." In obedience he accepts the call — "Speak, Lord; for Thy servant heareth." And by that acceptance his character is sealed evermore. "Samuel grew, and the Lord was with him, and did let none of his words fall to the ground. And all Israel from Dan even to Beersheba knew that Samuel was established to be a prophet of the Lord." We are not all called to be prophets, but we are called, in our varying ways, to minister to the Lord; and we may learn from this typical history how to recognise and answer our call.

We are apt to lead aimless lives, and shift the blame of them on to our circumstances; but circumstances, to a believer in God, are providential, and meant to determine and not to divert our aim. Parents' wishes, constitutional temperament, intellect, rank, wealth, poverty, obscurity, the books we read, the friends we form, family claims or the absence of them, sudden disasters, or unexpected opportunities in the opening days of life,— these are the things that decide for us the main outlines of our career. And it is very easy to imagine that they are all happy or unhappy accidents, importing at the very outset a character of chance into all that we do. But such a view is only born of the shallow philosophy that sees nothing in the universe but a chaos of shifting sand. And it is in the presence of such feelings that a belief in vocation comes to our help. For that belief gives us a clue to the right interpretation of our circumstances, and leads us to ponder over them with prayer. As we do so we are no longer content to drift idly before them, or to turn and go away in a rage because we are not bidden to do some great thing. The loyal acceptance of what may seem to us a lower alternative is often the first stage of some transcendent mission, and the perfect performance of insignificant duties may lead us very far in the spiritual life. Many of our material and intellectual surroundings turn out to be temptations of the kind in which we are bidden to rejoice, necessary trials of our faith, forcing us to make our choice between the reproach of Christ and the riches in Egypt. While the frequent frustration of our hopes, or ambitions, or affections, may lead us on to see how open failure is the very instrument of hidden success, and a broken heart a great vocation. In this way the stream of circumstance will guide, but never overwhelm us, if only we are awake to its providential character, as one among the many means by which God calls us to Himself—the external side of our vocation.

But external circumstances need for their interpretation the inner guidance of the voice of God; and to hear that voice we must be listening with the obedient expectation in which Samuel said, "Speak; for Thy servant heareth." It is too readily assumed that such interior calls come only to the favoured few who are predestined to exceptional careers. But many, we read, are called, but few chosen. And the reason is that only those few have been willing to listen to the call. We need not hear an articulate voice, such as bade Augustine "take and read." Yet kindred experiences even to this are commoner by far than most men dream. Augustine's intellectual friends might easily have explained that voice away; but it was the crisis of his history, and through that history it has echoed, and still echoes, with incalculable power in the world to-day. Doubtless, too, it might have been called an irrational and foolish impulse which led St. Francis to stake his all upon the chance occurrence of a passage in the Gospel at a particular moment of his life: still it was an impulse fraught with untold blessing for subsequent ages of men. In a word, these things are not accidents. They are ways in which God, the Holy Ghost, chooses the weak things of the world to confound the wise; flashing on the mind in an instant, through some chance thought, or sight, or sound, the conviction of His nearness, and the message of His will. If we listen in the woods in summer, the whole air, which at first seemed silent, is stirred with unnumbered echoes of bird and insect life; and in like manner to the spiritual listener, the awed silence of the human heart will grow quick with the voices of God. But spiritual listeners are few, and the great majority of men, after a momentary pause of uneasiness, dismiss these voices from their mind, as curious coincidences, or tricks of morbid imagination; perhaps even misquoting them in after days, to shake the confidence of nobler souls. "We too," they will say, "in our enthusiastic youth, were liable to such hallucinations, but we have outlived them now." Yes, and they should add, "We have outlived with them the spiritual vocation that might once have been ours."

But real as these inner intimations of the Divine purpose often are, they need to be received with care. And here again the case of Samuel comes before us. The voice which called him was interpreted by Eli. "Eli perceived that the Lord had called the child." And all our secret inspirations need a similar process of testing, in the light of our own experience or that of others. Their congruity with our character and circumstances, their relation to our own past prayers, the aspect which they present to unbiassed advisers of spiritual mind, their correspondence with what we know of the ways in which others have been led, the degree of their persistence under adverse conditions, are among the points to be considered as throwing light upon our vocation. And when such considerations coincide with and confirm the outward guidance of our circumstances, and the inward attraction which we believe to be Divine, we may go forward in the hope that the Lord is with us, and will "let none of our words fall to the ground."

There have been times when thoughts like these involved men in serious perplexity, as to the compatibility of divine election with the freedom of the human will. And great caution was then needed in their treatment. But our age, as a whole, has reacted from all such tendencies; and our danger lies, as we have seen, in the very opposite direction, that of doubting, or at least ignoring, a particular providence in human affairs. We tend to forget that not a sparrow falls to the ground without our Father; and that the very hairs of our head are numbered. We can hardly, therefore, in the present day insist too much upon the thought, that our choice and pursuance of a profession in life means our acceptance or rejection of a divine vocation.

What, then, is a divine vocation? It is a call *from* the world, in its evil sense, *to* God. It is a detachment from the one, and an attachment to the other. These are its two essential characteristics. First, detachment, or

K

sacrifice. When the rich young man was bidden to sell all that he had and give to the poor, the involved sacrifice was obvious. But though less obvious, the sacrifice need not be less real in the case of those whose undoubted vocation is to accept the responsibility of a great inheritance. To be called to assume early in life the serious attitude towards property which most men only acquire after years; to be daily accustomed to riches, and yet to be detached from them in heart; to forego luxuries which are in our power; to maintain the warfare with temptation, when temptation is fortified and aided by one of its most invincible allies—this is indeed to live a life of sacrifice. Or again, to be called to public life, and amid its manifold distractions remain free from party bias or personal ambition, pure in purpose, high in aim, setting the affections upon things above, not on things on the earth—this, too, is a life of sacrifice, not less intense than when we long for fame and are called to obscurity, or for action and are called to passivity of pain. And it is the same at whatever career we look.

We may drift into life aimlessly or selfishly, without much disturbing our ease; but no sooner do we view it as a divine vocation than we are at once involved in sacrifice; for we are at necessary issue with the evil in ourselves and in the world. "If ye were of the world, the world would love his own, but because ye are not of the world, but I have chosen you out of the world, therefore the world hateth you."

Secondly, attachment. Vocation is a call to God, and not merely a call to labour. It is a common mistake to regard our work as leading us to God, rather than God as leading us to our work. But the latter is the true order of vocation. God calls us to Himself, and then sends us to labour in His vineyard, bids us reap where we have not sown, makes us fishers of men. This distinction, though it may seem subtle, is of great practical importance, for it involves the whole question of the right relation between character and conduct, the spiritual and the moral life. If we sever our moral life from its spiritual root—its root in the Father of

Spirits—and confine our thoughts to any kind of merely moral practice, however noble, we are liable by degrees to be too absorbed in our work, to over-estimate its importance and our own importance as its agents, to be unduly discouraged by failure or sudden avocation, and finally to lapse into the favourite fallacy of a busy but irreligious age—the fallacy that excess of action can atone for defect of character. Meanwhile, our work itself will lack the note of perfectness which spirituality alone can give, and be either outwardly ungracious or inwardly unreal. Whereas if we regard morality as a function of the spiritual life, and conduct as the consequence and not the cause of character, the natural and necessary outcome and expression of the inner man, all things will fall into their proper place. For the work which flows instinctively from character is not only more perfect in kind; but there is, in reality, more of it. It has a wider and more varied scope. In fact, it is incessant; since a character is always working, and never more profoundly than in those moments of unconscious influence of which it is wholly unaware. The mere existence of a saint does more than the busy activity of many sinners. And, further, while action divorced from character contains no principle of growth, and at best can only increase in quantity, remaining monotonously same in kind, a spiritual character is for ever growing in refinement and intensity and grace, and consequently issuing in a higher quality of conduct. Bishop Andrewes made it a prayer that even his postures and his gestures might be informed by the Spirit of God. Hence we see the importance of viewing our vocation as primarily and immediately a call *to* God; as such, obliging us, by its very nature, to repent and purify our hearts, and follow after that holiness without which no man shall see the Lord; before pausing to inquire what work we are likely thereafter to be set to do. "My son, give Me thy heart" is the universal form of all vocation; nor can the spirit in which it must be accepted find a better expression than the well-known words—

> Nearer my God, to Thee,
> Nearer to Thee !
> E'en though it be a cross
> That raiseth me.

This is the essence of vocation; and it naturally issues in a reality and earnestness of life which nothing else can give. Without it men may be in earnest for a time, but their earnestness will rarely survive failure, much less such repeated failure as is our common human lot. They begin to have misgivings about the value of their work, or the possibility of its accomplishment. They have "scorned delights and lived laborious days"; and to what purpose has it all been? Their objects have not been realised, and perhaps were not worth their efforts. And so their work is at last given up, or cynically lowered in its tone. The writer or the artist does not inspire us as once he did. The politician is no longer what once he was. The enthusiasm of the man of science or the social reformer becomes acrimonious, and needs the stimulant of continual controversy for its support. It is not that head or hand have lost their cunning; but the heart has lost its hope. But the man with a sense of vocation is beyond all this. For he neither depends upon success or failure, nor doubts the real value of his work. Like the Pompeian sentinel, come what may, he will stay on duty till his guard is relieved. He is a man under authority, coming and going at another's will. He works not for achievement, but for obedience, and rests not when he is tired, but when he is told; and though his work may be unrewarded, he knows that it will be utilised, for there is no waste in the great household of the master that he serves.

Nor does this temper of mind, as is sometimes thought, lead to dull and mechanical working. On the contrary, the man with a vocation is the truest *individual*. For in his degree he reflects God, and no two beings can reflect God in the same way. The philosopher often laments the loss of scope for individual character, under the conditions of modern democracy and its massive modes of action; and the artist the loss of picturesqueness in a society which closely resembles the monotonous rows of uniform streets in which it dwells. But it is not modern life, but modern apathy that gives these things their sting. Indolence is always commonplace. Imitation is its favourite method. And the more selfish men become either in their personal or collective aims, the more drearily they resemble one another. The course of an unchecked sin may be foretold with accuracy, for its history has been repeating itself for ages; but the course of an unchecked virtue, never: it is full of surprises, for it is the development of a new individuality in the world. No two saints were ever alike. And this the man with a true sense of vocation feels. He gives himself up to God in confidence that the maker of the human soul alone knows the capabilities of his own instrument, and can alone bring out its music. And he is justified by the result. For latent faculties and unexpected powers emerge in him as time goes on, to the confusion of many an abler companion who far surpassed him in his youth; and by degrees his "peculiar difference" becomes a factor in the world, a fresh and original contribution to the variety and interest of life. Native individuality alone will not do this. It may start with a flash and a lustre, but succumbs in time to the deadening custom of the world, "the set gray life, and apathetic end"—one more instance of the epigram that "we are born originals and die copies." But vocation, while it emphasises our originality, supports us under its loneliness with the sense of being upheld from above. "Ye have not chosen Me, but I have chosen you, and ordained you, that ye should go and bring forth fruit, and that your fruit should remain." This thought that we are not choosers but chosen is the root of the whole matter; for the cause of that choice is love. And to be the object of infinite Love is to be the subject of infinite development.

These thoughts apply to all vocations. But to-day, when we are especially bound to pray for all those who are to be called to any office and administration in the Church, the vocation to the Christian ministry naturally rises before us. "Do you trust that you are inwardly moved by the Holy Ghost to take upon you this office and ministration?" are the solemn words addressed to those who are about to be ordained. These words should, through all the previous years of preparation, sustain the courage and increase the devotion of those whose purpose is already confirmed; while they warn waverers of the high destiny which they are tempted to decline. For many are so tempted and succumb to the temptation. Many who by the various influences of early life and education, or by the generous impulses of youth, have been led to view ordination as their goal, hesitate when they near their object, and finally turn away. But if circumstances are providential, and early impulses the voice of God, their vocation has already begun; and before daring to refuse it, they should examine very earnestly the grounds of their refusal. Are their intellectual doubts wholly unconnected with some pleasant sin, or desire for the liberty of sinning? Is not their sense of moral unfitness a call to render themselves fit? Are not the attractions of other careers, in their case, nothing but temptations? Is not theirs the condition of the young man whom Jesus loved, and yet who "made through cowardice the great refusal," when perchance in the power of that love he might have risen to be another St. John? And meanwhile what of the alternative careers into which these men stray? Are they, instead of being viewed as spheres of separate vocation, to be thought of only as places of refuge for the spiritually destitute, and entered upon with no more than the mere negative qualification of unfitness for other things? There is the life of teaching in a school, for example—one of the noblest of vocations. Shall a man blindly stumble into it, and presume—for it means no less—to feed the lambs of Christ, because he shrinks from the call to feed His sheep? And yet this is not an uncommon case; nor is this the only profession which, in like circumstances, is undertaken with like want of thought or hope.

Again there are degrees and stages of vocation—vocations within vocations. And in proportion to the zeal with which a man answers to his call to the clerical life, he will hear fresh calls, as that life goes on, to do or suffer more ; to go up higher, either in the normal direction of pastoral activity or in some especial field. There is much need, for instance, now as ever, for work in the field of theology. But " pectus facit theologum "—the heart makes the theologian — the heart that has been given to God. Intellect combined with mental tendency is not enough. The Christian student's is not a life of literary ease, directed to theological subjects. It was not so that Clement, Origen, Jerome, Athanasius, Basil, Gregory, Augustine, Leo, Anselm, Thomas, led the way ; nor so that their successors in after years have pursued it. The life of the theologian is before all things a life of prayer ; and often of wrestling, not only with the fiery temptations which beset us all, but with special and exceptional foes of its own. The crown of the Christian intellect has been called a crown of thorns. Theology is a matter of vocation. And then there is the missionary call, of which we hear from all sides of the need. We must not hastily conclude that because this vocation comes to some men early, it may not come to others later on. Columba had reached middle life when he was called through penitence to his place in the mission field. And then again there is the life of absolute and entire self-surrender—the "religious" life in its technical sense. Great and glorious as have been the fruits of that life in Christian history, it might have seemed impossible half a century ago to hope for its revival in the English Church. But it has been revived, and there is a call for its extension. In the work of this revival, as in so many spiritual works, since the day when Mary Magdalene was the first to proclaim her risen Lord, woman has been privileged to lead the way: woman, who, however many new and great vocations may be opened up before her in the time to come, will still find her highest mission in the life of silent sanctity whose influence and attraction shall lead other souls to God. Women, despite of obloquy, enmity, suspicion, were foremost in restoring the religious life to its natural place in our church. And there is a cry for men, in greater numbers, to follow in their train. But no amount of external necessity, no utilitarian considerations can effect this. The dedicated life is a distinct vocation, which all cannot receive; great alike in its present sacrifice and in its promised glory—the vocation to leave all here for Christ, and hereafter to be of those who sing the new song of the undefiled.

"These are they which follow the Lamb whithersoever He goeth. These were redeemed from among men, being the first-fruits unto God and to the Lamb."

Such are some of the ways in which God calls men nearer to Himself. But we must not let the thought of these high vocations, which perhaps never may be ours, obscure in our minds the memory that we have all of us some vocation : some destiny which we cannot possibly carve out for ourselves, but to which, if we only listen, God's voice will guide us in due time ; some path of sacrifice which, whether men name it secular or sacred, is our appointed way to find and to be found of Him ; some purpose of love, for which first He called us out of nothingness to life ; and to which, though we have wandered from it, He is waiting to recall us, if only we will cast aside our cowardice, and say, " Speak ; for Thy servant heareth."

# IX

# THE CAPTIVITY OF THOUGHT

*"Bringing into captivity every thought to the obedience of Christ."*—2 COR. x. 5.

WHEN a truth has become a truism, or, in other words, so familiar as to pass unheeded, no apology is needed for its restatement; and among such truths may perhaps be classed the obligation involved in the words of my text, the duty of systematic self-control in the matter of thought. No one denies it; but few realise the extent of its application, and the methodical discipline that it demands.

"The soul," said M. Aurelius, "is dyed the colour of its thoughts." And the many scriptural warnings to the same effect are too well known to need repeating. Not only the moral and spiritual, but the intellectual, and even the physical, life is determined by the nature of our thoughts, and we can only be free in proportion as the thoughts which thus determine our character are in their turn determined by ourselves, or self-controlled. And when we hear men disclaim responsibility for their intellectual views, it is a proof that they have not duly analysed the nature of the elements out of which mature opinions are gradually formed.

We are all at times familiar with the difficulty of banishing evil thoughts from the mind—thoughts of resentment, or anxiety, or impurity, or pride; and in the light of this hard experience are apt to consider the injunction to "bring every thought into captivity" as an impossible ideal. But it may be that the Apostle knew and meant what he was saying; and that if we recognised our responsibility for the whole of our thoughts, good, bad, and what are called indifferent, we should obtain an easier conquest over those that are definitely evil. For control means guidance as well as repression. We control not only with the bit and bridle, but also with the whip and spur. We cannot divert the mind from evil without converting it to good; and this involves discipline of the thinking faculty, even more than of the objects of thought.

Now the chief danger of the thinking faculty is lest it should lose its vital energy, its spontaneity, its freedom, and allow itself to be determined from without; as when we speak of men becoming the *slaves* of party, or of prejudice or passion; and there is consequent risk in every influence which weakens the active powers of the mind—its powers of attention, observation, selection, construction, recollection, and the like. For its native vitality once gone, it is the sport of each current of opinion, drifting like a log on the waters, to be cast away on any shore.

If this be true, there is much to make us anxious, both in modern education and the condition of modern literature.

In the first place, modern education is increasingly utilitarian. It aims more than heretofore at providing the mind with such definite kinds of information as are likely to be of immediate use in after life, or even in the still nearer future of an examination ; and naturally, therefore, presents knowledge in such ready-made shape and form as may most easily be assimilated by the pupil. Such a system is perhaps an inevitable product of the age, and has obviously many advantages. But it has one grave defect. It trains the receptive rather than the active capabilities of the mind ; it teaches men to know rather than to think, and results in a type of intellect that is well-informed, but weak. Of course this is only true of the average action of the system ; but after all that means its action over the majority of men.

Secondly, this danger is increased by the very nature of modern literature—its scale and the rapidity with which it is both produced and perused. Daily, weekly, monthly, a flood of fresh literature is poured from the press, of which the educated mind must take account. But in doing so, it is subjected to a rapid succession of impressions from without—facts, rumours, theories, criticisms, more or less ephemeral, which for the most part obliterate one another, and cannot fail, in the course of time, to impair the powers of recollection, of constructive imagination, and of general intellectual grasp. It is a well-known saying of Bishop Butler, that passive emotions grow weaker by repetition; and it should be remembered that this means they weaken the mind through which they flow; and meanwhile the very ability with which current literature is conducted rather increases than diminishes the risk in question, by rendering the exertion of independent thought apparently superfluous.

Here, then, are two influences eminently adverse to mental self-possession. And their significance consists in the continuity and subtlety of their action. They are always at work, and imperceptibly at work. And to realise their dangerous character requires an effort of the very faculty whose power of effort they slowly tend to undermine. Thus, if we are seriously to master our thoughts, instead of being mastered by them, to exercise a free selection both in the quantity and quality of the things that we shall think about, choosing what we really desire to the exclusion of all else, and so calling into activity the inner resources of the mind, we must begin by guarding against the insidious difficulty that besets us, from the enervating character of the intellectual atmosphere we breathe. Still this will be only the beginning of our task. The mind's power of self-control may be endangered not only by disuse, but by misuse. For the objects that we think about react upon our power of thinking, and insensibly but radically modify its action—

> As a lover or chameleon grows like what he looks upon.

Where, indeed, the objects in question are obviously evil we are at least aware of the fact, and to that extent upon our guard. But there is a large region of things apparently indifferent where we suspect no harm, and yet are liable to be mentally enslaved.

For example, there is great danger in that

increased specialisation of study which the progress of our knowledge necessitates, and the tendency of our education, as we have seen, materially assists. The intellectual dangers attendant upon this specialisation have been often pointed out by modern thinkers, and are less easily corrected than deplored. But it also involves a moral risk of bigotry and partisanship that will leave us no longer free. For exclusive familiarity with a particular class of facts and particular methods of inquiry induces a gradual inability to appreciate other methods and other facts; a blindness of which the victims are conspicuously unaware. What is often called the controversy between theology and science is an obvious case of this. It is really a controversy between specialists, more or less culpably incapable of entering into alien points of view. And this is only one, though a notorious instance of the degree to which special studies may bias the independence of the mind.

Then there is criticism: not the finer criticism whose work is more properly called "appreciation," but that universal tone of criticism which permeates the pages of the newspaper or review — criticism of politicians and their policy, of philosophers and their theories, of judges and their verdicts, of clergy and their utterances, of artists and their creations, of critics and their views. Incidentally this criticism contributes to mental indolence, by supplying us with thoughts ready-made. But beyond this it tends to foster a critical attitude of mind, which is fatal to the highest exercise of thought. For "we live," says Wordsworth truly, "by admiration, hope, and love." And the habitually critical temper is profoundly hostile to all these three. It is complacent and superior to the child-like grace of admiration, the spirit of wonder in which philosophy and faith alike begin. It is too familiar with men's faults and failures to retain much hope. And love, blind, mystic love,— love that hopeth all things, and believeth all things, and thinketh no evil, and vaunteth not itself,—love must be for ever a sealed secret from its eyes. The prevalence of criticism, therefore, puts the mind in a false position, subordinating its primary to its secondary functions, the more to the less important, intuition to reflection, construction to analysis; sometimes, it should perhaps be added, humility to pride.

Again there is the literature of fiction, of which the novel may stand for a type. Its influence for evil, as well as for good, is incalculably great in the modern world; and must be reckoned with as affecting us, at least indirectly, through its effect upon others, and consequently upon the public opinion of our age. The evils of excessive novel-reading are of course too obvious for present mention. But quite apart from these evils, the character and tone of this class of literature may colour the whole imagination, shape the forms of thought, determine the bent and cast of the entire mind. And this in various ways. Thus there is the romantic novel, which, if it appeals to a different audience from heretofore, by doing so has only amplified its range. Romance has its glorious aspect, but also its attendant shadow. It is the parent of those treacherous habits of castle-building and daydreaming, which look innocent enough at first, but release the imagination from control; and are only seen in their true colours when the dreams have become lurid, and the deeds done in the castle chambers are deeds of pride or shame. Then there is the literature of excitement, that we have grown accustomed to call sensational, including not only the sensational novel, but the sensational treatment of any topic in other forms of literature. It is a common fallacy to suppose that sensational literature is harmless, if its incidents and allusions are not immoral, in the miserably conventional sense of the word. But the real harm of sensational literature lies in its action on the nervous system, and is incalculably immense. For it not only issues in a thousand wretched forms of mental nervousness; but through these in disease and disorder of the senses and the sensual desires, reacting upon the whole nature of the mind. Once more, there is the realistic novel. Realism, of course, strictly speaking, is only the name of a method; but this method has been so applied by its exponents to the illustration of one aspect of life—the material—as to have become almost its synonym.  Hence its danger.  Realistic literature, for all its accurate detail, is in the deepest sense unreal.  It is untrue to nature, because it presents a part as if it were typical of the whole.  It selects a partial phase of all that is happening in the world—certain situations, certain kinds of character — and then says, "this is reality," this is life.  Whereas, in fact, a complete picture of life would present mankind as for ever struggling to rise above the level of its lower self; efforts of the few to raise the many; aspirations of the many towards the few: everywhere, indeed, earthliness, but everywhere, also, the salt of the earth; the flesh lusting against the spirit, but the spirit also against the flesh.  And the suppression of one element in this picture falsifies the whole, and presents the mind with a false standard and false canons of judgment upon life.

Such are a few examples of the indirect kinds

of agency which often, without our knowing it, impede and misdirect the mind; so that when we set ourselves to bring our thoughts into captivity, we find that our power to do so is no longer what it was. We cannot afford, therefore, to underestimate any intellectual influence on the ground that its operation is unseen. It is unseen but incessant influences, acting through the ages, that degrade the mountains and exalt the plains; and in like manner, unseen influences, acting through a lifetime, lift the human heart to heaven or lower it to hell. And hence it is in the region of unnoticed danger that our mental self-control must begin. It is there that we must learn the habits, grow accustomed to the armour, forge the weapons, wherewith to meet more open foes. For we have more open foes, and our success against them must depend upon our readiness to recognise and encounter them as such.

For example, there is literature that undermines morality, and literature that undermines faith; and even these owe much of their malignity to the disguises they assume, the plausible pretexts under which they steal upon us unaware. Directly immoral books may be easily detected, and therefore shunned; yet these are often played with, on the specious pretence of gaining experience, or the sham chivalry that refuses to condemn even vice unheard. They are played with, a spark falls, the imagination is aflame, the whole soul is enwrapped in conflagration; and though perhaps the fire may die down and be forgotten, the conscience is for ever seared. But a more extensive form of the same danger results from the prevalence of books which are of immoral tendency without being immoral. Many authors do not seem to have thought out their own first principles, or the possible consequences to which they may conduce; they have incorporated, perhaps unconsciously, the floating evil that is in the air, and would disclaim the extreme conclusions which more susceptible or logical minds cannot fail to draw from their works. The peculiar danger of such writing arises from the fact that it has easy access to all society, and cannot be avoided till it is already known, and its mischief half accomplished.

The treatment of writing that may undermine our faith is a far more complex problem, for no universal rule can ever be applied to its perusal; what is necessary, and even wholesome to one, being utterly harmful to another. But one thing is certain; such literature would not constitute the danger that it does if it were always approached with sincerity of conscience and earnestness of aim. It is the dallying with doubt in our unguarded moments; the influence of unworthy motives, such as intellectual pride, or the secret desire for an easier life; it is aimless curiosity, want of seriousness, indolence, indifference, that convert what are only intellectual difficulties into grounds of disbelief. The study, then, of such subjects should be regarded as a responsibility, not a pastime, and never undertaken without a sense of the tremendous issues it may possibly involve. There was probably no single phase of contemporaneous unbelief into which the mighty mind of St. Thomas Aquinas did not enter; but we know in what a spirit, and therefore with what a result. "Bene scripsisti de Me, Thoma."

Literature is, of course, not the only avenue by which thoughts enter the mind, but the principles which should guide us through literature will apply equally to art, to conversation, and to all our other sources of intellectual good or ill. The goal we are told to aim at is the captivity of every thought, and this needs a watchful survey of all the things whence thoughts arise. It will be our wisdom to accept guidance, in this process, from the expressed opinions of those who are more experienced or holier than ourselves; and the obedience which this may involve is no mean grace. But still external machinery cannot do our duty for us. Every man, in the last resort, must be his own censor of the press; educating his own judgment, and strengthening his own will for the task.

At the same time it must not be supposed that the work in question is merely negative.

It is necessary to dwell upon its negative aspect—the kinds of thought to be avoided, or to be accepted with cautious care—because the dangers which, as we have seen, beset us, are so insidious in their operation as easily to escape our eye. But this negative work is, of course, only a means towards a positive end; and can only be fully accomplished by keeping that end in view. Fulness and not emptiness is the destiny of the mind; self-development, not merely self-control. And accordingly the same Apostle who bids us cast down imaginations, and bring every thought into captivity, supplies us elsewhere with a description of how this is to be done. "Whatsoever things are true, whatsoever things are honourable, whatsoever things are just, whatsoever things are pure, whatsoever things are lovely, whatsoever things are of good report; if there be any virtue, and if there be any praise, think on these things." It is a sufficiently magnificent enumeration of the true objects of human thought; and in proportion as we rise to it, lower aims and unworthier interests will lose their hold upon the soul and fall away. For the contemplation of virtue is the true cure of vice. Great literature, noble art, true science, holy example, assimilate the minds of their disciples to themselves; and by successive degrees create indifference, distaste, dislike, disgust for all inferior things. But if they are to do this for us, we must make them our own, dwell upon them, meditate upon them, read, mark, learn, and inwardly digest them. And this will require an effort, conscious, energetic, and sustained. For we are not always immediately drawn to what is noblest, and loveliest, and best. We have often to learn to recognise it, and even then to learn to like it; and the discipline that must train our spiritual eye to what is good, whether in literature, art, or life, is not less serious than that which is needed to protect it from the influence of evil.

The field in which this discipline has to be exercised is intellectual, but the discipline itself is moral and spiritual, and only to be acquired by moral and spiritual means. The injunction to "bring every thought into captivity" would be a mockery, but for the addition "to the obedience of Christ." Prudential motives or natural aspirations may carry us a certain way, but they will fail us in those critical moments on which the issues of life depend, unless they are reinforced by the strength of the Christian power, and the splendour of the Christian hope. For the obedience to Christ includes both the negative and positive duties of the mind, its self-control and its self-development, and alone makes either possible.

In the first place, obedience to Christ means crucifixion. "If any man will come after Me, let him deny himself, and take up his cross and follow Me." We know this well enough as a general principle, but we do not always recognise the universality of its range, and amongst others, its intellectual application.

The watchful, earnest, patient struggle with the external difficulties, the unsuspected dangers, the evil desires of the mind, is a veritable crucifixion. In all cases it affects the very root of our character, and in some it is the main probation of our entire earthly life. As such, then, we must expect it, accept it, endure it, with all that it implies of interior withdrawal from the ordinary ways and opinions of men; and this we can only do through "Christ, that strengtheneth us," and "worketh in us both to will and to do of His good pleasure."

But, in the second place, we must remember that crucifixion is a means to an end—the negative moment, so to phrase it, of our spiritual development; and to bring our thoughts into captivity to the obedience of Christ, is to enlist them in that service which is perfect freedom, to divert them from all empty unrealities, in order to fasten them on Him who is the fulness of Him who filleth all in all. The objects of science—He created them, and they illustrate His thoughts. The visions of philosophy—He inspired them who is the light of men. Language and its literature is His vicegerent, for He is the Eternal Word. The creations of art are symbols of His beauty, and His incarnation is their crown. If there be any virtue, if there be any praise, it is due to His presence in the souls of men. This is the goal of our intellectual life, the final cause of our mind—to think on these things in such a way that they may lead us on to think of Him who is their source; that so we may desire, and by desiring prepare for, the day when "we shall be like Him, for we shall see Him as He is."

# X

# PRAYER

"Pray without ceasing."—1 Thess. v. 17.

Prayer, in the light of history, is a natural human instinct. Here and there, indeed, among races whom we are fairly entitled to call degraded, men may be found who to all appearance are without it. But such cases are exceptional, and it is begging a great question to call them primitive. For, however far we penetrate into the records of the past, we find it characteristic of man to pray. Prehistoric man used amulets which analogy connects with prayer. And from the dawn of authentic history man has always prayed. We unroll Egyptian papyri, and find them filled with forms of prayer. We unearth Babylonian tablets, and amid all their sorceries and superstitions there is prayer. We translate the ancient books of India, of Persia, or of China, and they too are replete with prayer. And in the face of facts like these, which modern research is daily revealing, the shallow scepticism which viewed religion as a creation of priestcraft is no longer possible. For we find the craving of our own heart confirmed by the induction of historic science, that wherever man has been he has prayed.

Yet many of those who often pray, and most, if not all, of those who seldom pray, would seem to have a very inadequate conception of what prayer really is. Petition, begging, asking, which is only one among many parts and aspects of prayer, is commonly mistaken for the whole. And the consequent notion that an answer must be looked for in the shape of some definite boon, leads at once to doubts and difficulties about the efficacy of prayer. Many of these doubts and difficulties would vanish if, instead of regarding prayer in one only of its many aspects, we looked at its essential nature. For prayer is in reality the breath of the spiritual life—the act, the habit, the instinct of inhaling that divine atmosphere in which our spirits live and move and have their being. Our bodies only live by imbibing food and air. Our minds only live by intellectual sustenance. And so, too, our spiritual nature needs spiritual support. And that support consists in intercourse with the Father of Spirits, and all that such intercourse involves. "O Lord, Thou hast searched me out, and known me: Thou knowest my down-sitting, and mine up-rising: Thou understandest my thoughts long before. Thou art about my path, and about my bed: and spiest out all my ways. For lo, there is not a word in my tongue: but Thou, O Lord, knowest it altogether. . . . Whither shall I go then from Thy Spirit: or whither shall I go then from Thy presence? If I climb up into heaven, Thou art there: if I go down to hell, Thou art there also. If I take the wings of the morning: and remain in the uttermost parts of the sea; even there also shall Thy hand lead me: and Thy right hand shall hold me. If I say, Peradventure the darkness shall cover me: then shall my night be turned to day." Our first thought as we lift our eyes to the Father of Spirits, is that we are thus awfully, intimately known — known as no earthly parent, no friend or enemy, has ever known us; known as we have never even dreamed of knowing ourselves. And intercourse with One who so knows us must on our part be almost superhumanly sincere. Yet this sincerity is not a thing to be acquired in a moment. It involves self-examination, and detection of our natural self-deceit; and all this is a work of time before it can become habitual; while without it our prayers will be only new forms of self-delusion; less gross, perhaps, but hardly less fatal than that of Louis XI. praying for leave to commit one more sin. For it is not mere intellectual sincerity that we have to aim at, but the sincerity of a sinner before Him who is of too pure eyes to behold iniquity—a sincerity which, even when it has done its utmost, must still cry, "Who can tell how oft he offendeth: O cleanse Thou me from my secret faults." In a word, we must be penitent in order to pray

Perfect truthfulness and heartfelt repentance—these, then, are the first conditions of the efficacy of prayer; and they cannot be summoned at will when we kneel down to pray, unless we carry them about with us as permanent elements of our life. Wrestling, watching, fasting, fainting, withdrawing into the wilderness, all its Scriptural accompaniments, imply that prayer is a thing of effort, an energy, a real work of the soul. And it is reported of the dying Coleridge, with all his depth and his intensity, that he had never known till the end of life how hard a thing it really was to pray.

Still, there is another side to the picture. Prayer may be hard, but it is natural to man; for man is a spiritual being, and his spirit gasps for breath. "My soul is athirst for God, yea, even for the living God." "My soul hath a desire and longing to enter into the courts of the Lord: my heart and my flesh rejoice in the living God." "For Thou, O Lord God, art the thing that I long for: Thou art my hope, even from my youth." "Thou that hearest the prayer: unto Thee shall all flesh come."

Doubtless these expressions are the utterances of saints; but they are inarticulately present in every soul of man. St. Augustine, after confessing the licentious pleasures in which he continually hoped for, but never found, his satisfaction; his ambition of eloquence and its rapid disillusionment; his vain wanderings through every phase of the current philosophy in search of truth; his broken heart at the death of friends; his yearly increasing self-contempt and passionate unrest; suddenly sees as in a lightning flash, and sums up the meaning of it all in the words, " O God, Thou hast made our hearts for Thyself, and they are restless till they rest in Thee." And many a man who is still struggling to satisfy his soul with one or another of the distractions which Augustine pictures, or slowly but surely sinking into that despair of satisfaction which leads on to moral cynicism and intellectual pessimism, to issue at last in some form of suicide decently disguised, owes all his misery to the simple fact that he is a praying creature who has ceased to pray. Yes; hard as it may be to pray, it is far harder not to pray; and while the difficulty of prayer diminishes as the habit of it grows, the difficulty of living prayerless only increases with increasing years, for it is nothing less than a contradiction of the universal law of nature, by which everything that lives is irresistibly impelled to seek the conditions of its own continuance.

Prayer, then, so far from being a mechanical attempt to put in operation calculable causes for the production of calculable effects, is the intercourse of spirit with spirit, person with person; and as such is as various in its forms, and phases, and moods, and crises, and helps, and hindrances, and interruptions, as is the complex social intercourse of our life on earth, differing only in intensity and awe. If we would learn, therefore, to understand the life of prayer, we must turn from the physical sciences and the analogies which they suggest; for the simple reason that they deal with a single department of life and thought—the department where things are weighed and measured and tested by appeal to the experience of sense:

and we must retire into the deeper region of personality, where freedom and holiness and love have their abode, and through that region the biographies of the men of prayer must be our guide, and foremost among such biographies the Bible. The Bible in its long list of spiritual heroes reflects for us every phase and vicissitude of the life of prayer, and its continual outgoing from the secret chamber of the individual soul to become a factor in the development of public events. Men sometimes think the value of the Bible may be diminished, because we have so enlarged our ideas of inspiration as to see that myth may be inspired as well as history, an editor as well as an author. But the true danger lies not in multiplying the vehicles, but in ignoring the fact of inspiration, as is the case where we allow our interest in critical analysis or picturesque description to blind us to the essential significance of the Scriptural " History of Israel "; which is to show us that men and nations have their true life in the spiritual world—the world whose motor energy is prayer.

Thus the very name of Israel carries us at once to the prayer of Jacob in the solemn crisis of his life, when the treacherous conduct of his youth rose up against him in the person of a defrauded brother, and he wrestled the long night through—wrestled with the awful nameless One, with tears and supplications, while the very sinews of his body shrank, till he had won for himself at last the new nature sealed by the new name.

Kings, soldiers, statesmen, patriots, prophets, priests are thus in turn unveiled before us. And each fresh portrait brings into relief some special aspect of the life of prayer; while all culminate in the history of Him "who was in all things tempted like as we are." His life from Bethlehem to Calvary was one unceasing prayer. And yet when it is drawing to its end, and we are admitted to the privacy of its closing hours, prayer is still a thing of agony and awful fluctuations. The calm "Father, I will" of the great Eucharistic prayer, is followed almost immediately by the agonised "not my will, but Thine be done." And then when

Gethsemane is over, and the cross accepted and the triumph won, and the words of royal absolution, "To-day shalt thou be with Me in paradise," seem to come to us from the conqueror already entering His rest, we hear the cry of one more conflict echoing through the darkness—a cry of more awful import than came even from Gethsemane, and then at last, but not till then, the life-long prayer is over.

Meditation upon such thoughts as these may make it easier for us to pray, by making the true nature of prayer a more intelligible thing to us, and leading us to see how profoundly it is often misunderstood by men who would dictate to us its theory, while themselves utterly unversed in its practice. Still the removal of intellectual misconceptions will not of itself create the life of prayer. It prepares the way by showing us the difficulty, and yet the necessity, of prayer, and what we are to expect, and what not to expect, from it. But still there remains the moral effort to be made and to be sustained. The body needs physical, and the mind intellectual exercise, yet neither of these can be maintained without considerable effort. And it is no reflection, therefore, upon the naturalness of prayer to say that it can only be acquired at a like cost. Yet this is what men often forget, and in consequence of their forgetfulness lose first the habit, then the faculty, then the belief in prayer.

Hence the necessity for our sacred buildings, our ceremonial liturgy, our recurring hours, our warning bells. They arouse men to the fact that prayer is a life, a thing of continuity, for ever going on, and needing its daily exercise in order to its due development. The prayerful man may possibly have risen above all thought of forms, but the prayerless man is still below them, and needs invitations to their use. For how but by forms and practices are all the variety of habits acquired, out of which the fabric of our mental and moral and social life is built? We learn to write or paint or discourse music by setting ourselves a copy or form, till, by its repeated imitation, we have made the art our own. We acquire athletic or intellectual aptitudes by setting tasks before us, till by frequent repetition the laborious effort has passed into a second nature. There is one way, and one only, of acquiring a habit, and that is the repetition of its acts; yet, till a thing has become habitual to us, we are not in the full sense free to do it. Our freedom must be the flower of slavery, and will grow upon no other root. It is no derogation, therefore, from the spirituality of prayer to say that the man who will retain, still more the man who must return to, the prayerful habits of his early days, cannot afford to dispense with some degree of that moral compulsion which the recurrence of times and seasons and ceremonial forms involves. Spirit, as we know it, acts only in and through material agencies, which in their turn react powerfully upon its own development. In proportion as we forget this, we degrade the material world into a dead thing—a thing without a soul—and so come to dissociate secular from sacred things, to the infinite harm of both; for if we will not spiritualise our secular, we shall come to secularise our spiritual life. The two must be welded together, intermingled, intertwined. And this is the work of prayer, which, finding the necessity of times, and places, and gestures, and postures for its own assistance and its own expression, comes by degrees, not, as we inadequately phrase it, to be independent of them, but to universalise them, to recognise them everywhere and always, making the world one sacrament, eternally suggestive of spiritual things. Our Lord sets us this example by bidding us lift our thoughts to heaven when we contemplate the clothing of the lily or the lowering of the sunset, when we see the lightning flash from east to west, or hear the wind blowing where it listeth; and again more solemnly when He points through the veil of our bodily diseases to the sins of which they are always the symbols, often the effects; while He consecrates an ablution and a meal, the two necessities of our daily life, to be the witness, through the ages, of His spiritual presence among men. If we looked more in this way on life and nature, we should find the whole air full of church-bells ringing us to prayer. The piece of undeserved good-fortune, the sudden evidence of another's love, the rush of yearning in the presence of scenery, the flush of affection for some absent or neglected friend, the momentary pang that warns us of our mortality, the anguish of a parting, the memory of an ancient sin, the daily contents of our newspapers, with their deeds of heroism, shameful exposures, piteous disasters, sudden deaths—each of these as they flash through the soul and are gone, may wing a prayer to heaven, short, intense, inarticulate, but strengthening the spiritual life, making its successive efforts easier, and investing the recurrence of religious hours and times and seasons with a more and more welcome light, quickening our formal prayers, and expanding and extending them when they are over, and filling up their intervals, and linking them together, and making their scope universal. And as prayer thus grows upon us we shall see how far removed it is from that spiritual mendicancy whose efficacy men have strangely proposed, yet in all apparent seriousness, to test by experiment—experiment, that is, upon God. For the more we come to feel our own ignorance and impotence in presence of the mighty forces among which we live and move, the more completely shall we feel that our only safety lies in praying that for us, in us, through us, our Father's will may be done. Affection, meditation, praise will gather round this central prayer, but the essence of them all will be the offering up of our own weak wills to God: that, according to the law of all true sacrifice, we may find them again in Him, we may receive them back with usury, cleansed, enlightened, strengthened by that

> Living will that shall endure
> When all that seems shall suffer shock.

The analogy of human friendship may indeed suggest that, as intimacy grows, petition, though rarer, may be more prevailing. But we must remember that into the higher mysteries of this awful intercourse none can enter but by experience; and the only competent critic of the power of the fervent prayer of a righteous man, is the righteous man who fervently prays.

For God's will, which we pray may be done, is, after all, no impersonal law. It is the will of a personal Being who in the secret chamber of our soul reasons, expostulates, explains, warns, guides, attracts us to Himself. And this is the thought which may best sustain us to pray and not to faint. If we are created to seek intercourse with God, it is because He so created us, or, in other words, because He first desired intercourse with us, and therefore endowed us with its capacity. It is an attribute of our creation, and therefore a purpose of our Creator. And as Christians we know, what even as men we could not but hope, that the purposes of our creation are purposes of love; and that our every effort to fulfil them will be more than met by Him who first loved us and gave Himself for us, and who has left us the picture of the father who, when his sinful son was a great way off, saw him, and had compassion on him, and ran, and fell on his neck, and kissed him.

Yes; above the thought that we are known, with all its awfulness towers the thought that, despite that knowledge, we are also loved—loved through all the disguises that conceal us from ourselves or others; loved through all our temptations, our sorrows, our sins; loved through all our ineffectual wanderings away from love; loved with a love which, because it is all-holy, must at times appear to sinners strangely, imperiously stern; but all the while desires to have fuller fellowship with us in prayer, and to say to us at the last, "Ask, and ye shall receive, that your joy may be full."

## XI

## THE INCARNATION OF THE WORD[1]

"The Word was made flesh."—St. John i. 14.

THE Incarnation of our Lord has a bearing upon the problems of science and philosophy, the history of matter, and the history of mind, as well as upon the personal hopes of the individual soul. In other words, it is a theological as well as a religious truth; and intimately as the two are connected, they must still be kept apart in the mind. For the common tendency which there is to confuse them is responsible for many of the intellectual difficulties which now, as of old, are hindering the acceptance of the faith. Now, as of old, the religious missionary whose whole being is devoted to track moral evil to its hideous haunts,

[1] Reprinted from the *Expositor*, 1886.

and there fight it in its grosser forms — to rescue and renew and guide the souls of sinners Godward — naturally tends to emphasise the undreamed, unhoped, unexpected, miraculous character of Christian grace; the strangeness of our salvation, so far beyond all we looked for. And so the Incarnation comes to be regarded as an isolated exception to the order of the world, a Divine afterthought, if we may say so reverently, consequent upon human sins.

But the age is scientific as well as practical, and science knows nothing of isolated exceptions. It is not possible that men whose bias is to view things from the intellectual side, should not be alienated from the Christian message, the Christian life, the Christian hope, by the popular travesties of Christian theology, to which the insulation of a few doctrines, for homiletic purposes, and the disproportionate insistence on them, has gradually given rise.

We cannot therefore, in the present day, recur too often to, or dwell too strongly on, those portions of the teaching of St. Paul and of St. John which exhibit the Incarnation as the predestined, and in that sense as the natural, summary and climax of the material creation,

> Cent'ring in Himself complete what truth
> Is elsewhere scattered, partial, and afar.

"By Him all things were made"—the atoms, which we call ultimate; the myriad modes and forms and fashions into which the atoms are transmuted and built up; heat and light and electricity; the world of colour and the world of sound; the courses of the stars, the strength of the mountains, the raiment of the lilies, the beauty and the wonder of bird and insect life, the uncouth animals, the mind of man—"and without Him was not any thing made that was made." So far all Theists are agreed. But mere Theism does not satisfy the mind. The closer we look into the material world, with its resistless, omnipresent, inextinguishable energies of life, the more we feel that we are in the presence-chamber of a power that is Divine. Nature does not bear the stamp of a machine created by a far-off God, and then left to its own working. Theism, if it would not shrink up into Deism, must go forward into Pantheism;

and yet, to be consistent with itself, it cannot. But the Christian creed continues, "In Him was life." The Creator of the world has not deserted it. He sustains it. He indwells it. And the forces that have gathered suns and stars out of the formless mist, and shaped them for use and habitation, and peopled them with life, and supported and sustained that life through all its gradual development, "till at the last arose the man," are part of the working hitherto of Him who is the life.

And that Life was the light of men. Above all other forms of energy towers the thought of man—slowly building up societies; evolving, as we say, a moral consciousness; refining age by age upon the moral ideals of its past; issuing, as leisure increases, in art, philosophy, and science; culminating in the pangs of martyrs and the ecstasy of saints. And through all this process we believe that that Life has been the light of men. The Inventor has been explaining His own machinery, the Artist exhibiting His own pictures, the Author re-reading His own book; the Creator leading men by slow degrees to learn the meaning of His own creation, by teaching them first to discover and then to co-operate with its laws. "He left not Himself without witness," says St. Paul. Socrates and Plato, not less than Moses and Isaiah, dimly descried personalities beyond the horizon of authentic history, such as were the Buddha, Confucius, Zarathustra, and all the unknown, unhonoured pioneers of early thought, are among those through whom, "at sundry times, in divers manners, God spake in times past unto the fathers"; and all the legitimate developments of art, all the verified discoveries of science, all the yearnings of our race for larger liberty or lovelier life, are manifestations of the Life that was the light of men—ways in which for ever He is coming to His own.

Finally, "The Word was made flesh, and dwelt among us." The thought is presented by St. John as a climax. Matter in its successive gradations, from the conflict of atoms to the body of the saint, had been expressing with increasing clearness the character and attributes of its Creator. Reason had been yearning to reduce its material embodiment from stubborn resistance to obedient freedom, and at length in the fulness of time the two currents coalesce. Matter becomes at last an adequate expression of its Creator. God is at last revealed to His creation in material form. And the Incarnation, once accomplished, throws a "supplementary reflux of light" upon all the ascending stages of the world's antecedent evolution.

For the fact of the Resurrection, as attested, preached, appealed to, by St. Paul, is too plain an event of history to be possibly ignored, and the Resurrection, once accepted, proves the Incarnation to have been a reality; independently of the undoubted truth that our more sympathetic modern criticism tends increasingly towards the conviction that no combination of, or refinement upon, the thoughts of antecedent thinkers, could have invented the Incarnation if it had not actually happened. Here, as in all other cases, philosophy is the interpreter of history: it never has been, it never can be, its creator. But if we thus view the Incarnation as no interruption of previous development, but as the climax, the summary, the fulfilment of all nature's dim auguries, of all philosophic aspirations, of all that prophet and king had desired to see and had not seen ; predestined, we may well believe, as did the Scotist theologians, independently of human sin— secular thought and the secular world, as it is called, assume for us a new significance. Our Lord did not cease to appeal to the teaching of the lilies, and the corn, and the sunrise, as if its need were superseded by His being the very truth. He only reveals it to be more nearly one with Him than men had before suspected, by such phrases as "I am the Vine," "I am the Shepherd," "I am the Bread of Life." He does not abrogate the Roman law, but only points to its emanation from above. He says expressly of the drift of previous Hebrew history, "Think not that I am come to destroy : I am not come to destroy, but to fulfil."

So that, on whatever side of us we look, we see in Christianity not so much a circumference within which is truth, and outside which falsehood, as a centre of attraction towards which all that is lovely and of good report is for ever drawing nearer, till approximation becomes prophecy. Thus the face of external nature, with its loveliness of form and colour, and all its endless harmony of action and repose, speaks to us not only of an Artist who designed it, but also of an indwelling Spirit which sustains and animates its every part, and is revealed with increasing clearness as we ascend in the scale of creation, from the mystery of the mountains, to the life of the trees that clothe them, and the motions of the beasts that haunt them, and the senses, the hearts, the brains of the men that look upon them and love them; as sculptured expression is surpassed by painting, and painting again by music, and music when it can rise no higher, bursts, as in Beethoven's great last symphony, articulate into song. And we cannot but feel in the presence of such a fact as this, that all the forms of nature-worship which we find among savage races, much more the refined Pantheism of later days, point to a truth which professing Christians are often apt to underrate. They cannot be summarised and set aside as the merely fanciful creations of a superstitious or poetic temperament. They are only the inadequate expressions of a legitimate human instinct whose natural satisfaction is the doctrine of the "Word made flesh." Our judgment of the modern pantheist will vary with the nature of the causes which withhold him from his allegiance to the faith "as it is in Christ." But we must remember that there is an element of Divine truth which we believe in common, and an element which we are unfaithful to our Master's teaching if we overlook. Or again, if we look below the surface, from nature's aspect to her operations, we see more there than the contrivance of a mighty machinist. For the great machinery lives, throbs, pulses with an energy which is ever at work controlling, transforming, quickening the stubborn atoms into versatile, obedient ministers to the free activity of man. Can we wonder if the miracle of matter hides all else from its too eager student, and he stops short in some form or other of materialistic creed? We may pity him, with humility, for all the hope he loses; but before we blame him, we who have not blanched our cheeks or bleared our eyes in the dark mine, we must ask ourselves severely what use we have made of his life's labours. The more we learn of the importunate reality of matter and of its intimate connection with the things we are accustomed to call spiritual, the more necessity we see for the Incarnation, if religion is ever to be adequate to human life in its entirety; and the more reasonableness in its sacramental application to our souls. This much, at least, the materialist ought to have taught us about God's world, and he can only have taught it by patient obedience to God's law of learning. We are bound to accept his teaching with thankfulness as seeing in it more than he ever dreamed of, but with trembling for the account of it we must one day give as representing the life of our brother laid down for our enlightenment. Physical science for the Christian means nothing less than a fresh flood of light. It is at our peril that we complacently treat it as if it were only one more foe.

So, too, with the civilisation by which we are surrounded. It does not follow because we deny that Christianity could ever have been evolved out of the mere action of those complex forces which go to make up what we call secular civilisation, that it is not largely indebted to those forces in every age, as beyond question was the case when it first began to overspread the world. We are familiar with the thought that the Roman roads, and the Roman law, and the universal language were part of a providential "præparatio evangelica"; but many to whom this is a commonplace, shrink from the more important fact that the ideas which paved the way for, and the phrases which embodied the very cardinal truths of, our theology in early ages, were prepared in the schools of Athens for the work they were afterwards to do. But for that theology, which men have not scrupled to represent as a paganised corruption of the simplicity of the Gospel, the Gospel would never have been preserved in its primitive integrity to after ages. For that theology was nothing more than the intellectual insistence upon the reality of the fact that "the Word was made flesh." And its authors were sustained and emboldened in their work by the conviction that it was the point to which the same eternal Word had in all philosophy and prophecy been guiding the minds of men.

But if the eternal Word was working in the thinkers of the early world, He cannot be less present among secular movements now. We often hear men speak as if with the advent of Christianity, the Spirit of God had retired from the extra-Christian world. But the very thought is a contradiction in terms. True, it is impossible in a complex age like ours to disentangle the different forces that are at work within society; and many a movement that seems extra-Christian may have come from a Christian source; but even if this were not so, the principle would still remain that every good gift and every perfect gift cometh from above. The increase of political liberty, with all the opportunities for development and discipline of character, which self-government involves, the humaneness of modern law, the spread of sanitary science, with its consequent moral blessings, the mitigations of war, and increasing amity of nations, the extension of intellectual culture and the recognition of its value, all are due, through whatever agency they seem to come about, "to the Light that lighteth every man coming into the world."

This view of the Incarnation as the climax to which all life and thought lead up, has naturally found its most emphatic expression in intellectual ages, and at the Ephesus or Alexandria, the intellectual centres of their age. At times when thought was not, and the vital energies of the Christian Church were concentrated in a death-struggle with the moral evil of the world, her speculative mission would lie in comparative abeyance. But never, perhaps, before has it more needed reassertion than in an age which looks at all things in the light of their evolution.

Our Lord Jesus Christ stands forth as the head and summary of that material creation through whose gradual development He had all along been preparing for Himself a body—

man made at last in the image of God. He stands forth as the final utterance of those eternal verities which philosophy had all along been struggling to express with stammering tongue and lisping lips—the Word made flesh. He stands as the goal in which all human progress finds its possibility, its meaning, and its end—the Way, the Truth, and the Life. He is immanent, as we say, in all creation; but none the less He is its Creator, and as such not only through all, but above all, God for ever. As long as we hold this truth firmly we cannot over-estimate the reality of His partial presence in materialism, in pantheism, in secular civilisation, and in all the various imperfect forms of moral conduct and religious creed. And it is our duty as Christians never to under-estimate that presence, not only because no part of God's revelation of Himself to men can in the long run be ever neglected with impunity; but also because it is only by these less direct methods of approach that many souls are capable of being led to Him at all. While, on the other hand, we may never rest content till we have done all we can to lead men forward from the lesser to the larger light, from the vision through a glass darkly to the vision face to face.

For what our Incarnate Lord is to the universe considered as a whole, and to humanity in the mass, He is also to the individual persons of which humanity consists. And the special mission of the Christian, as distinct from all other teachers, is to bring men one by one into personal relation with their Lord. For "personality" is the highest mode of existence known to our experience. The material of our bodies, and the thoughts of our minds, drift through us like a stream, and are gone we know not where; but the personality, the "I," within us remains from the cradle to the grave, self-identical, self-conscious, independent, irresponsible, alone—the one supreme reality of which we are completely certain, and of which any solution of the universe that is to satisfy must take account. It is nothing to us to know that God dwells in matter, and moves in thought, and moulds the varying purposes of men to His own ends, unless He is in some relation to these "personalities" of ours, with their importunate claim to be ends in themselves, not instruments used and thrown aside. But persons can only really be united to a person, as we see in our daily life. It is not in the amusements, or the business, or even in the duties, which occupy our bodies, or brains, or wills, that we really live; but in the contact which they involve, and the response that they call out from our fellows, our friends and dear ones, persons like ourselves.

Hence the solitary significance of the Incarnation. On the one side it was a revelation, fuller only in degree, of the God who had been working hitherto in the material, the intellectual, the moral world. But on the other it was a revelation, different in kind, that God was not merely an impersonal "drift of tendency," nor supra-personal, in such sense as to obliterate His personality, but a Person, and as such, One in community with whom all human persons were destined to find the satisfaction of their complex being. This it is which differentiates

Christianity from other creeds. It is not only obedience to a law, or even following an example, but union with a Person.

Now the point in which persons touch is the will. We may think like others, or act like others, without being really one with them. We are only one with them when we will what they will, and because they will it. And so the end and object of the Christian's will is to be conformed to the will of Christ. In the early stages of our life-long development, that will of Christ may only appear to us as an inexorable moral law, convincing us of sin; but as we struggle on, the commands of the law melt into the accents of a voice within us, more and more articulate the more they are obeyed; and duties are done easily, and sanctions become needless, for it is God that worketh in us, both to will and to do of His good pleasure. And therefore Christian holiness is no less attainable than the more limited aims of conduct which we are so often advised to pursue; because we believe that the Holy Spirit dwells within us, to quicken us into living manifestations of Himself.

And from this follows our much-controverted Christian doctrine, that the intellectual is dependent upon the moral and spiritual life. Particular branches of knowledge may be successfully acquired apart from the general character of the individual man who pursues them. But if the complete illumination of the intellect is only to be found in union with Him who is at once its Author, its Object, and its Light, and personal holiness is the necessary condition of that union, it follows that only he who "doeth the will shall know of the doctrine," despite of the familiar fact that many a distinguished thinker is actively anti-Christian either in conduct or in creed; while many a sincere Christian lives and dies in intellectual ignorance. For what is the secret of scientific success? Humility, the man of science will be the first to tell you, in receiving the revelation of nature's laws; obedience to those laws as one by one they are revealed to him; patience in the face of failure; perseverance to the end. But all these are moral qualities of God's ordaining, and precisely as he observes them the man of science will become to us a discoverer and teacher of the truth of God, and worthy of all the reverence which God's instruments deserve. It is only when such an one stops short of, or denies, what we as Christians must believe to be the legitimate end and issue of his message, that we follow him no longer. He has taught us much which we lesser men should never have learned without him, and it is not for us to pry into the hidden causes of his further failure. Our Master's call is plain to us. "What is that to thee? Follow thou Me." But diffident as we are, and ought to be, in maintaining our position against intellectual superiors, when we think what moral effort that superiority has cost, it is far otherwise when we face the misbelief of the average world. For one man such as has been described, there are ten thousand misbelievers who are what they are simply because they "do not the will." Pride, sloth, self-seeking, above all, sins of the flesh, in whatever shape or form, blind the eye, dull the ear, deaden the understanding to the things of God. And when men plead intellectual uncertainty in defence of immoral life, they will find, if they only look within, that they are mistaking effect for cause, and the source of all their malady is an evil *heart* of unbelief. Sin keeps them far away from the Person of Jesus Christ, and therefore from the Truth which is His thought embodied in the world. On the other hand, the Christian, however ignorant he may seem of things external, is only beginning the process of his knowledge at the other end; from centre to circumference, instead of circumference to centre. He feels his personal nearness to the mind of Christ, and studies first to learn the dealings of that mind with his own soul. For there he sees the meaning of the bright ideals of his early life, and of all the joys and sorrows that have chequered his career—the bereavements, the frustrate purposes, the slow detachment from the world, the strangely occurrent whispers of consolation and of warning, the deepening insight, the increasing peace—till he can read through his whole history the special providence of One who loves him, and whose character and ways of working are revealed in that love.

There is an indifference to earthly knowledge which only comes of indolence; but there is an indifference which belongs to those who have chosen the part of Mary, and cannot for a moment be away from Him they love. So the great politician, or philosopher, or poet is known to the outer world by the work that he has done; but his child, his wife, his friend, who know the human heart within him, are content in that great knowledge to leave all else alone. It is this interior knowledge of the mind of Christ that the Christian, in proportion to his progress, feels himself to possess; and once possessed, it must thereafter give a new bias to his life. He will sympathise intensely with all the secular schemes and systems which in any way throw light on life and further the well-being of his fellow-men. But his own mission is to bear witness, at whatever risk of misconstruction, to the existence of the more excellent way. He welcomes the signs of progress in the dark places of the earth; but progress is slow, and time is short, and souls are dying every day; and "the one thing needful" is to bring them to the knowledge of the love of God, declared to us by Christ His Son.

But there remains yet another constituent of our human personality, beside our reason and our will—the body that is the instrument of all our thought and action, the wondrous garment interwoven with the very fibres of our soul, the messenger for good and evil between us and the world that is without. The more we learn in these modern days of the mystery of matter, of the ethereal subtlety of its elemental structure and its infinite capacity for spiritual expression, the more instinctively we feel that it is not destined to be done away. It is too wonderful, too beautiful, too real to have been created but for waste, by One who bids us gather up fragments that nothing may be lost. And what are these bodies of ours but the very flower of the material creation, adequate to every impulse of their animating soul? Is there no greater fate for them than meets the eye? So far nature leads us; but if we look then to the Word made flesh, we feel that our natural instinct is more than justified

—for we see there a human body become the dwelling-place of God, and exhibiting, as a matter of history, in the few glimpses of its risen life, those infinite new capacities of our dim prophetic dreams. And the wisdom of the early Church becomes apparent in the grim tenacity with which, when philosophy meant idealism, and the secrets of matter were all unexplored, she clung to the reality of the human nature of her Lord. For only through the reality of that human nature can this last element of our personality, the body, rise to communion with the Eternal Word. There is a solidarity in the world of matter, linking its particles each to all; and individual things in their seeming distinctness are, when viewed from the material side, only the ripples of an ocean upon which they rise and fall. Each partial movement thrills the whole of it, and to touch it in a point is to touch it all. To this fact we owe much of the dark moral taint that we inherit from the days of old, but all the efficacy of its Christian antidote. For the leaven of the Incarnation leavened the whole lump. And in taking flesh upon Him, and transfiguring it by dying, the Word came into new contact, not only with the few in Palestine whom He breathed upon and sighed over, and healed by the trailing of His garment and the imposition of His hand, but with the human body everywhere, and its modes of material affection — sanctifying water to the mystical washing away of sin, consecrating bread and wine to holier purposes of sustenance, hallowing symbolic and ceremonial teaching, deepening the parables of nature and the significance of art. Yes; by His Incarnation we are all brought nearer to Himself; but contact is not communion. Many may touch and yet few be healed. Of bodily as of mental union with Him, the gateway is the will. For the will and not the body is the source and seat of sin. If the will is unholy, our nearness cannot but increase our alienation, as discord in a family is worse than with foreign foes. But if the will is holy, light and life and love flow into us through a thousand sacramental avenues from the risen body of our Lord.

By every channel, therefore, through which our personality radiates, we are called into communion with the Person of the Word made flesh; and the climax and completion of that communion is love. For love is not a function of part of our being, but of the whole. All other relations between men are in a measure abstract—they are concerned, that is, with their actions, or their thoughts, or their utility, as partners, colleagues, fellow-workers, employers, masters, slaves—with reference to some object that lies outside themselves. But if we love men it is for their own sake, because they are what they are. For love, and love alone, rests in its object as an end.

In appealing to our love, therefore, God appeals to our whole personality; and in revealing Himself as Love, He reveals His presence, along the ages, in all the yearnings of the human heart—to guide men to the one home in which alone they could find rest.

"To comprehend with all saints what is the breadth, and length, and depth, and height; and to know the love of Christ, which passeth knowledge," is the privilege only of personal religion—a vision to elect souls in pilgrimage among desert places of the unitive way. The humbler province of our theology is to tell those who have not seen it that for them, too, the vision waits.

In the deepest, in the fullest sense, seeing only is believing; but in an age like ours, of keen inquiry, we may lead many to come and see, by showing them that Christianity includes and finds a place for the affirmative assertions of all the other creeds; while by rejecting their negations, their exclusion, that is, of it and of each other, it is more comprehensive as a theory of the world, and therefore presumably more true. And in doing this we are not acting in any spirit of extorted concession, but reasserting the primitive doctrine, that the Eternal Word who created all things has been present from the beginning in the material world; in the course of philosophic thought; in the secular progress of mankind; in the wills, in the minds, in the bodies, in the whole persons of His saints; revealing more fully, in each new stage of universal evolution, "the mystery, which from the beginning of the world hath been hid in God, who created all things by Christ Jesus: to the intent that now, unto the principalities and powers in heavenly places, might be known by the Church the manifold wisdom of God, according to the eternal purpose which He purposed in Christ Jesus our Lord."

# XII

## THE RISEN LIFE

> "If ye then be risen with Christ, seek those things that are above."—COLOS. iii. 1.

ST. PAUL is emphatically the Apostle of the Resurrection. His earliest Epistle opens with the thought of it. His latest utterance as Paul the aged is "Remember Jesus Christ, risen from the dead." Death and life, mortification and quickening, burial and resurrection, are the burden of his preaching alike in the intellectual universities of Greece, and amid the manifold miseries of the great metropolis of Rome. Everywhere and always he asserts, insists upon, illustrates, argues for, bursts into highest eloquence over, the thought of the Resurrection. And few there are among us, however unversed in Scripture, who have not felt our heartstrings thrilled by the language of St. Paul, in that sad hour when, with broken hearts and tear-dimmed eyes, we stand beside the graves of one after another whom we have loved and lost, longing for a fuller measure of His mighty confidence who said, "O death, where is thy sting? O grave, where is thy victory?"

"If ye then be risen with Christ, seek those things that are above." St. Paul is addressing all baptized Christians, as being already risen with Christ; and inasmuch as the death of the body has not yet passed upon them, the sense in which they are risen is from sin. But we shall miss the whole force and power of his appeal if we lapse into supposing, as men so often do, that our resurrection from sin and our Lord's resurrection from death are meant to be connected only by a metaphor; in other words, that they are compared, and not united as effect and cause. Our Lord's resurrection from the grave is no greater miracle than His being man, and yet absolutely sinless. His power over sin and His power over death are, like the heat and the light of the sun, two radiations of the self-same energy—either of them containing evidence of the presence of the other, either of them justifying His own claim to be the very God, the central source alike of holiness and immortality. And because He is divinely, creatively Holy and Immortal, He can and will make His people holy and immortal too. But while in Him the two attributes are in reality but one, in us the creatures of time there lies a life-long day between them. First we hear His voice saying, "Thy sins be forgiven thee," and afterward "Arise and walk." Once to have heard the first voice is a pledge that we shall hear the second. For once to have felt within us the victory over sin, is a proof—an infinitely stronger proof than any philosophic speculation ever gave—that we already possess the quickening, immortalising Spirit that will not suffer His holy ones to see corruption. "If the Spirit of Him that raised up Jesus from the dead dwelleth in you, He that raised up Christ Jesus from the dead shall quicken also your mortal bodies through His Spirit that dwelleth in you." It is this confidence which makes St. Paul view our two resurrections so closely together that he speaks of them in places as virtually one, and addresses Christians as already risen *with* Christ, that is, not *like* Christ, but in, and through, and by, the actual presence of Christ within them.

Such a doctrine, nowadays, is often mocked as mystical; another name, when so applied, for utterly unreal. But never was the mockery more ill-judged than now. For we have long ago abandoned the stupid attempt of earlier ages to test a thing's reality by the evidence of sense. Our highest modern conception of reality is force or energy; and force is an invisible thing, known only by its results, the distance it can travel, the weight that it can raise, the work that it can do. We Christians, then, are not irrational, when, conscious of a work done within us which no philosopher, however great, no physician, however skilful, no loving care, no wise advice of father, mother, brother, friend, no self-reliance, no proper pride, ever has effected or ever could effect, we call that work superhuman, and point to it in evidence of a real cause within us, which must be superhuman too. "I live; yet not I, Christ liveth in me."

And so the Apostle continues, "Ye are dead." Precisely as a vigorous human vitality resists, rejects, sloughs off, destroys the germs of disease in our bodily organism, so the vitality of Christ within us will gradually kill out "the desires of the flesh and of the mind." "Your life is hid with Christ in God"—hid, that is, from the outer eye, but containing the promise of its future glory, as certainly as the seed that is hid beneath the soil will one day put on the loveliness of the rose or lily, or the grandeur of the oak. "Dead to the world," "Hidden with Christ," "Destined to glory," are only three descriptions of the self-same fact, that if we are really Christians "Christ liveth in us." And it is needful we should pause upon that fact till it is fully realised, for nothing else will give us strength to quit the sophistries of the world, the seductions of pleasure, the cravings of ambition, and lead the risen life, seeking those things which are above.

Nowhere is this more obvious than in that great region of life to which St. Paul first calls attention in the words following the text, the region which is overshadowed by the sins of the flesh—sins which the Apostle, knowing how easily they creep upon us, if once allowed the cover of euphemistic disguise, never names without enumerating openly in all their coarseness. Pandered to by many of the fashionable forms of art; fostered by the easy luxury of the age in which we live, they are ruining souls to-day as they ruined ancient Greece and Rome. To what do these sins owe half their power, but to the whispered suggestion, or the explicit evil teaching, that they are irresistible because they are natural? For the materialist who views man as merely the most complex animal, there is indeed no other alternative to this; though many a materialist, like the great Roman poet, is conscious that his moral instincts revolt from the conclusions of his creed. But far other is the teaching of St.

Paul. He points to a human body sitting on the right hand of God, and bids us there behold what an high destiny flesh is heir to, nothing less than to be "conformed to the image of His Son." And if this is our destiny, this is our true nature. For the "state of nature" which men dreamed of a century ago has long taken its place among the figments of the past. And science has now taught us to recall the truer view, that in a world where all develops, the true nature of each thing is not to be seen in the germ it starts from, nor even in the successive intermediate stages of its progress, but in the perfection of its final end. The nature of the seed is to become a tree, of the child to become a man. And so the true nature of this corruptible is to put on incorruption, and of this mortal to put on immortality. And the law of all development, which we can now so clearly trace, is that the lower capacities shall fade away as higher functions are performed, lesser organs become atrophied as larger are matured. "The seed which thou sowest is not quickened except it die." "When I was a child, I spake as a child, I understood as a child, I thought as a child: but when I became a man, I put away childish things." So far, therefore, from being unnatural in the true sense of the word, the mortification of our earthly members, even though it sometimes involve the plucking out of the right eye or the cutting off of the right hand, is strictly in accordance with the universal law by which alone created beings rise to higher things. The sole difference between us and the other orders of creation is, that what they do obediently, we habitually grudge to do, from the "law of sin which is in our members, warring against the law of our mind." No man can feel the deadly nature of that war within himself more intensely than, as we know from his own description of it, did St. Paul. And yet he was enabled to exclaim with full assurance, "Thanks be to God, which giveth us the victory through our Lord Jesus Christ"—*through*, not, that is, by a fictitiously imputed, but by a really imparted, righteousness, due to the "Spirit of God dwelling in us," "bearing witness with our spirit that we are the children of God," "helping our infirmities," "making intercession for us with groanings which cannot be uttered," "strengthening us with might in the inner man," revealing to us what things God hath prepared for them that love Him, in the heavenly places, where Christ sitteth at the right hand of God. It was the consciousness of this Divine indwelling which enabled the Christians of early ages, to rise above the floods of license, that were sapping the foundations of the Roman world, and raise, for the example of all who have come after them, a standard of heroic purity that can never be surpassed. And the Lord's arm is not shortened. "Jesus Christ is the same yesterday, to-day, and for ever." We, too, when temptation presses from without and from within, if only we will meet it in His power, and His alone, shall be more than conquerors through Him who loved us.

But the Apostle passes on, by a natural transition, from personal to social sins. For unrestrained appetite, with its necessary consequence, covetous desire for the means of its gratification, is, in the last analysis, the source of all social disorder. And the men who a century ago set the example of regarding bodily indulgence as natural to man, were perfectly consistent in representing his natural state as one of unintermittent warfare with his kind. And yet even heathen philosophy rose far above such shallow views. Man, said the greatest of Greek thinkers, is "born to be a citizen." Civilisation and not savagery is his truly natural state. St. Paul takes up the thought, which was current in his time, and invests it with a deeper meaning, and lifts it into larger light, when he reminds us that we are "fellow-citizens with the saints," and that "here we have no continuing city, we seek one to come." And as he had pointed to Christ as the Saviour of the individual body, so he points to Him again as the Head of the true body politic, before whom the inequalities of earthly life all fade away; "where there is neither Greek nor Jew, circumcision nor uncircumcision, Barbarian, Scythian, bond nor free: but Christ is all, and in all." That is our social goal and destiny, to be built up into the spiritual city, of which Jesus Christ is the head corner-stone. But our social no less than our individual resurrection awaits its manifestation in the world beyond the grave. Earnest enough we have of it in the works which the Christian spirit has slowly been accomplishing as the ages pass along—the vindication of the dignity of womanhood, the passing away of slavery, the higher tone to which society and policy are slowly being raised. But its glorious realisation cannot come about till sin has for ever passed away, and there shall be no more death. St. Paul, like his Master, proclaims the ideal of society, but forbids the premature attempt to reach it by unspiritual means. The man who could say of himself, " Who is offended, and I burn not ? " was not one to think lightly of the miseries of slavery, and yet he sends back the escaped slave Onesimus, content with bidding his master thenceforth treat him as a brother. And so he bids children be obedient, and parents considerate; wives submissive, and husbands loving; servants thorough in their service, and masters just. And all this because we live in direct, immediate relation to Christ, while our relations to each other are only secondary, and through His will. Our place, our condition, our circumstances, our various limitations, come from Him, and point to the vocation for which He destined us before the world was. "For whom He did foreknow, He also did predestinate." And therefore whatsoever we do, we are to do it "heartily, as to the Lord, and not to men." Now all this is as full of teaching for us as for the Colossians. The problems arising from domestic discord, from social inequality, from national antipathy, never pressed more fiercely for solution than to-day. And partisans on all sides would gladly see the Church of Christ identify herself with one or another of the many systems of secular conservation or secular reform. But this is not her mission, nor ever can be. For secular systems work from without inwards. The mission of the Church is to work outward from within. Secular systems deal with men in masses. The mission of the Church is to individual souls. Secular systems attack crime against society. The mission of the Church is to cure sin, the root of crime.

Secondary agencies may remove temptation, and limit the range of evil, by controlling its outward exhibition; but all this will not regenerate the world, unless the recesses of the soul be reached ; and that, and that alone, is the province of the Church of Christ. The instincts of our being do not deceive us when they point to a social ideal where no faculty shall lie unexercised, no capacity want opportunity, no true joy need to be foregone, and where the only inequalities of station or reward shall arise from inequality of duty done. And it is to fit us for such an existence that the Church labours to convert, to edify, to fortify individuals soul by soul. The fact that our social duties are correlative, and that it is hard for a servant or master, a husband or a wife, to continue in a course of duty which does not meet with its due response, does not affect the obligation which lies upon them to persevere. If all men acted out the precepts of the Sermon on the Mount, the kingdom of heaven would come near to being realised on earth. If one only enacts them in a world where they are counted foolishness, martyrdom may be his destiny, but none the less his duty; and this is only possible through the communicated energy of Him who is not only our far-off ideal, but also our very present help in trouble; not only the Finisher but the Author of our faith. Whether, therefore, we regard our destiny from its personal or social side, it is the presence of Him who is the Resurrection and the Life within us that alone can make its fulfilment possible, and assure us that we shall not be disappointed of our hope. And there is a further practical power in the new shape which the Resurrection has given to that hope itself. The resurrection of the body is not a mere theological truth, appealing to the intellect; it is a thought which gives our hope a new power over the heart and life. Till the first Easter morning the keenest thinkers of our race, however earnestly they longed for a future life beyond the grave, had been unable to conceive of it, except as a shadowy disembodied state, wanting in all that could give reality and substance to the thought; and the body with all its beauty, its wonderful expressional capacities, its intimate, immediate sympathy with our sorrows and our joys, the yearning heart, the speaking eye, the clinging hand, came to be regarded as a prison-house, confining and contaminating the purer soul; while others, in their natural revolt from the felt unreality of such a view, were driven to conclude from the close communion that exists between soul and body, that both must perish together, and that there was no immortality at all. And in the presence of such conflicting opinions, the practical hold upon an after life faded, dwindled, died away from the minds of the great mass of men. But the Resurrection has changed all this by bringing home, not to a few speculative thinkers here and there, but to the poor, the simple, the wayfarer, the humble man of heart, the truth that these bodies of ours are what they instinctively claim to be, essential to the completeness of our wondrous personality, as well as to our intercourse with all whom we live amongst and love. And every fresh light that science throws upon the marvellous nature of that which we call matter—the subtlety of its structure, its mysterious versatility, the omnipresent energy of which it is the vehicle and vesture—all this gives a new force to the natural analogies to which St. Paul appeals in illustration of the risen body with which we shall one day "be clothed upon."

THE END.

www.ingramcontent.com/pod-product-compliance
Lightning Source LLC
Chambersburg PA
CBHW021827230426
43669CB00008B/888